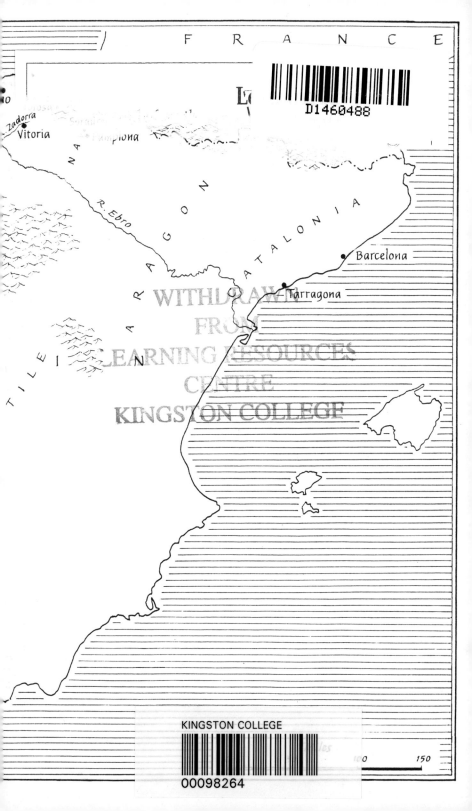

F R A N C E

D1460488

Lo

Zadorra
Vitoria

Pamplona

N A V A R R O

R. Ebro

A R A G O N

C A T A L O N I A

Barcelona

Tarragona

T I L E I

N

100   150

DOUGLAS'S TALE OF THE PENINSULA AND WATERLOO

DOUGLAS'S TALE OF THE PENINSULA
AND
WATERLOO

by

JOHN DOUGLAS

(former Sergeant, 1st Royal Scots)

Edited by

STANLEY MONICK

LEO COOPER
LONDON

First published in Great Britain in 1997 by
LEO COOPER
an imprint of
Pen & Sword Books Ltd
47 Church Street
Barnsley
South Yorkshire
S70 2AS

ISBN 0 85052 565 9

A catalogue record for this book is
available from the British Library

Printed in England by Redwood Books, Trowbridge, Wiltshire

Contents

Introduction and Acknowledgements

In his history of The Royal Scots A. M. Brander makes a brief reference to the memoirs of one John Douglas, who served for some years as a Corporal, and later a Sergeant, in the 3rd Battalion and fought with it at Walcheren, in the Peninsula and at Waterloo. The memoir is entitled *Douglas's Tale of the Peninsula* and spans the years 1809–17. It ends with the return of the battalion from the Army of Occupation in France for disbandment at Canterbury in April, 1817.

The memoir may be described as a monograph with many of the characteristics of the picaresque novel. It is episodic in form, making no serious attempt to present a detailed account of the battles of which the author is writing but rather to provide a view of events as seen through his own eyes. One of his aims in writing the memoir was to bring home to those who had no experience of the soldier's life and hardships on campaign just how much the marching infantryman had to endure for his country's sake.

Douglas was a well-educated, articulate and literate man who was a shrewd judge of character and of all that went on around him – a most unusual man to find in the ranks of an army largely recruited from the poorest levels of society among whom illiteracy was common and educational standards extremely low. His memoir is contained in a leather-bound volume of 172 pages of which the first thirty consist of a scrupulously researched history of his regiment. These are not reproduced in this book which is concerned with Douglas himself. The text is written in a fine and completely legible copperplate handwriting, a clear indication of his educational background and possibly of the five-year apprenticeship which he had completed just before he enlisted on what seems like a sudden whim, despite the fact that his friends 'came forward most handsomely with their purses to set me up in business on my own account'. Although there is no definite indication of the date at which the memoir was written, the fact that Douglas refers to published work that did not appear until the late 1830s suggests that he was writing some twenty-five or thirty years after the events described took place, possibly in the middle of the 1840s.

John Douglas was born in Lurgan, some twenty miles from Belfast, in about 1789. He came from a distinguished and aristocratic lineage, dating back to the first Earl Douglas of Drumlanrig whose title dated from 1358 and whose descendants featured prominently in Scottish history, the title finally passing to the Dukes of Hamilton in 1761. However, there can be little doubt that Douglas himself was born into a more modest branch of the family, well removed from those aristocratic links, but who nevertheless had the resources to give him the education that he had clearly enjoyed and to put him through his apprenticeship. The date of his death is not known but there is an interesting clue to the fact that he was still alive in 1848. His Waterloo Medal and Military General Service Medal, bearing the clasps Busaco, Fuentes De Onõro, Salamanca, Vittoria, San Sebastian, Nivelle and Nive, are now in the South African Museum of Military History in Johannesburg. The General Service Medal was only authorized in 1847 and issued in the following year. No posthumous issues were made so that many of the names appearing in the memoir are missing from the medal roll. Douglas was certainly a strong and very resilient man, for, despite having nearly lost a leg at San Sebastian, he was back in the battalion at Quatre Bras and Waterloo, so we may fairly hope that he lived to a good old age. The rims of both his medals are inscribed with his name in the rank of Corporal, so it is clear that he had not been promoted Sergeant by the time of Waterloo. However, in the Epilogue (page 105) he speaks of a 'fellow Sergeant' whilst at Canterbury (March or April, 1817) so it seems likely that he was promoted while in France, after the battle.

Douglas was a natural storyteller and raconteur, so the memoir makes wonderful reading and gives us a word picture of life in the Peninsula that no plain work of history could hope to provide. The episodes he describes range from the horrific to the farcical – from the rape of Busaco to his own encounter with a drunken naval Master-at-Arms. While his description of life on the march and in the field leaves little to the imagination in terms of the suffering and hardships which he and his comrades endured – desperate hunger when the Commissariat had failed to keep up with the army, the agonies of marching mile after mile barefoot when no new boots were available, sleepless nights spent soaked to the skin and lying on the bare earth under the stars after a hard day's march in pouring rain, and nights on which, despite some form of tentage, they awoke with their hair frozen to the grass – his tales of battle sometimes seem curiously matter-of-fact, written almost as if it was all something of a horrendous game, all part of the day's work, yet invariably reflecting that marvellous soldier's sense of humour without which the stress of battle could not long be endured. From time to time, however, he underlines the extreme dangers they faced and the stoic courage with which the British line would advance against the French guns and musketry in perfect order, despite the heavy casualties, or the fearful carnage inseparable from siege warfare. A man of deep religious convictions and a strong sense of natural justice, he felt extremely bitter at the way an ungrateful nation treated its old soldiers when their long years of service and sacrifice were over, often leaving them disabled or in poor health and unable to find work, yet receiving little or no financial recompense.

Apart from the two world wars of the 20th Century, no war in our history has yielded a more extensive literature than the war in the Peninsula. There are a great number of well-written memoirs and histories from the pens of officers of every seniority, but memoirs of the quality of *Douglas's Tale* from a soldier who served in the ranks are rare indeed and enable us to see the war through entirely different eyes.

Douglas's text has been reproduced as it was written. Editorial interference has been strictly confined to the inclusion or excision of a word or phrase which was found necessary in the interests of clarity. Similarly, because Douglas had little love for full stops or semi-colons, the text has been repunctuated in some places, again in the interests of clarity. Douglas's nine chapters have been compressed into six and section headings to indicate a switch of scene or subject have been introduced.

To provide some historical continuity and give a background to the events about to be described, a short historical note has been introduced at the start of each chapter. The Chapter Notes are only intended to clarify points in the text or to explain the significance of some situation or remark to the reader who has no previous knowledge of the military history of the period. Douglas used a small number of footnotes. These have been included amongst the Chapter Notes and endorsed *Author's Note*. A short Select Bibliography has been included for the use of the reader who wishes to study the campaigns in more depth or to learn something of the organization, equipment and tactics of the British armies under Wellington.

The editor is grateful to his former colleague Mr H. R. Paterson, Curator of Museums, The South African National Museum of Military History, Johannesburg, for valuable assistance and advice in the preparation of this book and for giving him access to the letter written by Mrs A. W. Douglas, great granddaughter of John Douglas, to the Museum in 1986. Much of the biographical detail on Douglas is derived from it.

He also acknowledges with gratitude the valuable detail on Wellington's armies and campaigns gleaned from the following principal sources: Correlli Barnett, *Britain and Her Army 1509–1970* (1984); A. M. Brander, *The Royal Scots* (1976); *The Dictionary of National Biography*; Sir John Fortescue, *History of the British Army* (1912); Michael Glover, *Wellington's Army* (1977); Philip J. Haythornthwaite, *Wellington's Military Machine* (1989); *The Journal of the Society for Army Historical Research*; A.T.C. Mullen ed. *Military General Service Medal 1793–1814* (1990); H.C.B. Rogers, *Wellington's Army (1979)*.

S. Monick
March, 1997

Prologue

The question, 'What is the reason that you do not write an account of your life?' has been so frequently put that I came to the resolution of committing a part of my travels to paper in order to save myself the trouble of narrating by piecemeal the hardships to which soldiers are, or were, exposed, trifling though they may appear. I trust that they will not, even at this remote period, be found altogether unworthy of notice, as it is my intention of relating whatever came under my notice with all the accuracy my memory is capable of at the same time. It must not be supposed that I intend to enter into a lengthened detail of the operations of the different Divisions, Brigades, etc which composed the British Army on the Peninsula, but simply to relate what I have been an eye witness to, and for the accuracy of which I trust there are still some Old Peninsular veterans in existence that can, if they would, vouch for the genuineness of the narrative. At the same time, if any error be laid down, I shall feel obliged by any of them pointing out the mistake that it may be rectified.

Chapter One

Enlistment and My First Campaign

In March, 1809, the British Government learned that a French naval squadron was anchored in the port of Flushing on the island of Walcheren, in the estuary of the Scheldt. Furthermore, the French were constructing docks at Antwerp to provide a base from which expeditions against the English coastline could be mounted. At the instigation of the Admiralty, it was decided to send a joint naval and military expedition, consisting of some 40,000 men and over 600 ships, under the command of Lieutenant General the Earl of Chatham, to capture Walcheren and demolish the new docks.

By 15 August the islands of Walcheren and South Beveland and the port of Flushing had been seized, the French having retired to the mainland. However, before an attack on Antwerp could be mounted, Chatham's troops were struck by a virulent epidemic of what was then known as Walcheren fever (malaria). By the end of August Chatham had decided that his rapidly falling strength, at a time when the French were being heavily reinforced, gave him no option but to abandon the expedition and return to England. The effects of the fever, as Douglas himself testifies, were long-lasting and even three months later about one third of the troops in the force were unfit for duty.

*   *   *

I being apprenticed to a trade against my inclination served 5 years faithfully with credit to myself and gain to my master; at the expiration of which my friends came forward most handsomely with their purses to set me up in business on my own account, but

3

in a great measure saved them the trouble by taking the coach for Belfast.

I Join the Royal Scots

From the first Regiment that offered I took the shilling to serve His Majesty in the 1st or Royal Scots, and to secure the bargain got attested on board the *Fanny* brig, a regular trader, and landed in Liverpool just as a number of the sick and wounded arrived from the funeral of Sir John Moore (or the battle of Corunna) where the 3rd Battalion lost on the retreat and in the battle 250 men. Nothing of moment occurred on the march if I may call it thus being sent from Liverpool to London by the canal.[1] This was marching at ease. We joined the Regiment then quartered at Chelmsford in Essex. The first salute I got with a number of others was being ordered to Hospital for the scratch.[2] I reasoned, I expostulated, I appealed to the Surgeon of my being clean but to no purpose, as it was a Regimental order that all recruits must, clean or unclean, undergo a sweat in the blue blankets.[3] To hospital I had to go, and there it took me 3 days and as many nights over my first military lesson. On emerging from this den, where the main diet was skilly I found I had what was not easily got rid of, a good appetite. Having got over marching drill with a pretty good grace, firelocks were introduced and having been in the Yeomanry I understood the use of them and how to handle these instruments a little better than my rustic neighbours in the same squad. This didn't escape the hawk's eye of the drill sergeant, who stepping up quietly enquired what regiment I had been in. Young as I was, I sounded his meaning and soon put him right, not without his suspicion as to my being a deserter.

It was now June 1809. The 3rd Battalion being well recovered at the battle of Corunna, got completed with a draft from the Fourth Battalion, consisting of 1 drum and 450 men, of which I made one. This put the Battalion in a state fit for service. We marched for Portsmouth ere I got dismissed from drill to join the Expedition designed for the island of Walcheren, commanded by the Earl of Chatham.[4]

The march to me was rather novel and I confess I felt a secret pleasure in seeing strange places, and in hopes of visiting others of which I had read much about.

The march ended without incident and for the first time on Southsea Common I became an inmate of a curious house. Here we were brigaded with the 5th and 35th Regiments. At this time

4

the landlords in England were compelled to furnish a good dinner and supper for 1/4d. In some cases, particularly along the Portsmouth road they were greatly imposed upon, not on account of the number of men quartered on them (which were unavoidably numerous at some stages) as the ignorant destruction which was practised on them to such a degree, that I have been astonished how they could keep a house over their heads. In general I have seen dinners provided that were both plentiful and of the best quality, and at which it was vexatious to see men, who to my knowledge when at home (that with the exception of Christmas and Easter) flesh meat never crossed their mouths, yet these and such like were the only men to find fault with dinners that were fit for any man in existence to sit down to.

During our sojourn here ball practice was the regular breakfast weather permitting. One morning a tailor belonging to our Company, not much accustomed to the use of arms, shot off all the fingers of the front rank man's left hand. I shall never forget Lieut Col Hay[5] upon that occasion. 'By G—', cried he, 'he will be a terror to ourselves and not to the enemy.' However, he brought the man along with us to Flushing, and sent him home with the first batch of wounded.

Hay was a very strict disciplinarian, and did not bear the best of names among the men. Take a specimen. In the Spring of 1809 the 3rd and 4th Battalions lay together at Chelmsford, and something like children of a family, they did not agree well together. Even the officers got tainted with such nonsense. The 3rd Battalion considering themselves superior to the 4th, it so happened that a man of the 4th Battalion Light Company, being on a spree, was taken by the picket in a state of intoxication, and snatching the pike (or halberd)[6] from the Sergeant struck him on the head.

This no doubt was a very serious crime, and was as seriously handled. The man being confined, reported and tried was sentenced to 800 lashes by Col. Hay, he being the senior commander. The man received 775 lashes without so much as asking for a drink of water. He then ordered him to be taken down and, addressing the 2 battalions, or the man, he says, 'Now Sir, I would sooner flog you for giving insolence to a Lance Corporal than for striking an officer, for that is the link in the chain by which the whole army is fastened.'

At length, all things being ready, we embarked, the left wing[7] on board the *Eagle*, 74 with the left wing of the 5th Foot; the

5

right wing on the *Revenge*, 74 with the right wing of the 5th. I heard many old soldiers say (having more experience than I) that a soldier could not be punished with sailors' cats[8], but we were soon confirmed that this was not the case. A Corporal (to whose lot it fell to unravel the mystery) having had a dispute with one of the Midshipmen, got reported to Captain Rowley of the *Eagle*, who ordered a parade, read a Section of the Articles of War against mutiny and desertion, tied him up to a grating, and served him out with 3 dozen lashes and the loss of his stripes. The poor Corporal, considering himself not fairly dealt with, wrote to Col Hay in the *Revenge*, stating his grievance and particularly dwelt on being punished with sailors' cats. The Col takes a boat and over to the *Eagle* he goes and acquaints the Captain with his errand, when a parade was ordered. The Col taking out the ex-Corporal's letter stated, 'So, Sir,' addressing him, 'you have written to me complaining of being punished with sailors' cats: and by god, if you do not behave better in future, I will hang you with sailors' ropes.' Thus that question was set at rest, though I dare say not to the satisfaction of all concerned.

The Walcheren Expedition

At length we sailed for our destination, the Island of Walcheren. The coast, and the River Scheldt, is not easily navigated by reason of shifting sand-banks. If I mistake it not 'twas on the 29th July 1809 we came to an anchor off the island. The appearance of the shore was one continual sand hill, and from the deck of the vessel it appeared to the naked eye as if the infantry were drawn up, but this proved to be large beams of timber driven in to break off the surf. This, with matting of straw fasted on the beach with pins of wood, prevents the sand from being washed away, for a breach in the bank would be the destruction of the Island, as I dare say the flat surface is 20 feet below the surface of the sea.

On Sunday the 30th the *Caesar* 74 and the *Eagle* got foul of each other owing to the bad anchorage. Cabin windows, bird cages, etc were floating in all directions, while the tide running so rapid whirled our boats about regardless of either helm or oar. At length we got clear of the eddy and stood in for the shore. I think the landing at Flushing was one of the grandest sights imaginable. The Ocean as far as the eye could reach seemed to be covered with Men-of-War, Frigates, Sloops, etc while the boats, with the troops, kept their line as correct as possible, the large vessels as it were in the background, while the Brigs, Schooners, gunboats, etc lay close in shore with their gun ports open ready to fire to cover the landing. The troops had orders as soon as the boat touched the ground to take their ammunition under the left arm, firelock in the right hand, jump and wade ashore, form line and prime and load. Lord Paget[9] in a boat was the first to land, and running up a sand hill he fired a pistol. This was the signal to make for the shore. As a matter of course we expected to be engaged even in the water. This was rather novel, not that all novelties are attractive, yet it was not destitute of a joke. In the stern of our boat sat Major Hill, who had on a huge pair of boots (not wishing to get wet) that reached nearly the length of his thigh. He considered himself as safe as insured on getting on shore dry, but unfortunately a great rough-spun fellow of the name of Dixon sat next to him. When the boat struck each and all made a spring for the shore at once, but Dixon's foot somehow struck the Major's and the first part of him that touched the water was the Major's head. In he tumbled body and sleeves. In any other place this would have been sport, but in the present case, with Jack Frenchman before us, it rather spoiled the fun. However, we fished him out, not altogether without a smile, nor could he suppress a smile himself.

We landed safe and sound, loaded and advanced up the beach, but no enemy made their appearance. Towards our left a 2 gun battery let fly some shots, and the 71st had a sharp skirmish in a wood. We halted on the sand hills that night, which proved both cold and wet, and could scarcely obtain as much fire as to light our pipes.

It happened that my comrade was a native of the island and was taken as interpreter to General Graham[10], one of the drunkenest rascals in existence. On August 1st we advanced towards Flushing, the main body keeping close by the shore, while the flank companies[11] drove in the enemy. We now came in full view of the town, being in column of companies at wheeling distance, and coming in range of the guns of the garrison they seemed in no way sparing of their shot and shell; but not having our proper range the greater part of it passed quietly over. One shell struck the centre of our column and, exploding, did a great deal of mischief. It came our company's turn to relieve the skirmishers and off I went on my first cruise. We had not proceeded far when coming round the left flank of a hill which had been thrown up in front forming a dyke, at the extreme right of which stood a flagstaff, we became exposed to a destructive fire of musketry

7

from a picket house and hedges round an orchard, together with round and grape[12] from the town to which we were exposed, and in less than half-an-hour left us minus 1 lieutenant[13] and 35 of the rank and file. Not a man in the company did not bear the marks of the balls through the different parts of his clothes. The first man I saw fall happened to be my front rank man named Dixon, who fell or rather sat down, and moved no more. On the bugles calling us back, I was in the act of loading when the tuft was shot off my cap, and on the instant of turning round a ball struck the leaf of the pouch[14] but no matter. In all the hurry of retreat, I stopped to examine poor Dixon, but where the ball had struck him I could not discover, as there was no blood to be seen. The 95th relieved us keeping the enemy in play while the entrenching tools were sent for to break ground. The shells from the town annoyed us very much. We now had to content ourselves with keeping them in proper bounds and opening the trenches, and be assured 'twas ticklish enough work. On the night of 7th August the French sallied out to destroy a 15 gun battery and six mortars.

The attack was principally directed upon our own advanced pickets. The Royals[15], 5th and 35th Regiments, with detachments of the 95th and King's German Legion[16] received them with such a salute as forced them to retire with considerable loss in killed, wounded and prisoners.

Captain Webber Smith, with 2 six pounders had done great execution upon the enemy with a few rounds of spherical case shot, as we could distinctly see the lanes made through the column by each round. At length our guns opened fire and in a few days all the enemy's batteries facing our works were silenced. The reserve were sitting one day on the side of the mound in rear of the guns then at work, listening to the shot and shell passing to and fro. Just in front and not more than a dozen yards off was a deep hole similar to a bog hole where turf has been taken from, and was now in the act of being filled up by a fatigue party of the 26th Regiment, one of whom was resting on the head of his spade when a musket ball struck him on the forehead and down he tumbled lifeless into the boghole. I often considered this one of the most curious shots I ever knew, as there was no enemy in front, nothing but the sea. The hill where 15 twenty-fours[17] and 6 mortars were playing was but a few yards on his left, and that was the only point from which a ball could come. 'Take that man to the surgeon,' said Col Hay. 'He is dead,' was the reply. 'Then

8

go on with your work, it is only a chance shot.' One of the artillery drivers[18] was coming along with a load of ammunition, seemingly regardless of the shot which was ploughing the earth around him, when one of them struck his horse and carried away one of the wheels of the wagon. He very deliberately dismounted, examined the extent of the mischief and then taking a pistol he tamed the horse by sending a ball through his leg; then shouldering his saddle bags he marched to the battery with the utmost composure.

The Siege of Flushing
The bombardment of Flushing was truly a grand sight and if there is a beauty in destruction it was here amplified. I have counted at night 15 shells and rockets[19] in the air at once. It is almost incredible the distance that shell can be thrown by such short pieces.[20]

The bombardment was largely directed from the boats[21] along-side and it was truly amazing to observe the distance and precision with which they fell onto the town.[22]

On the 13th we drove the enemy completely into the town and advanced the trenches, not without some trouble and loss. A curious circumstance took place on that occasion. One of the grenadier's wives by some means got smuggled on board, and I believe was the only woman on the expedition. Her name was Ross, a smart little woman. In the hurry of driving the enemy into the town, a good number got shut out, as the bridges were drawn up before all were in, and of course were made prisoners.[23] I saw the same woman with an entrenching shovel on her shoulder take charge of 6 prisoners and march them safe to the rear. It is curious that a small thing will turn a ball. Lieut M'Kenzie having a few guineas in a purse stopped a ball that must have proved fatal. Though he was greatly hurt his life was spared at the expense of a few shiners scattered about.

The enemy on the 15th thought they had enough of it and hung out the white flag. Terms were offered and accepted, the garrison to march out with the honours of war. Thus Flushing fell, and to this day it is my firm belief that had it been garrisoned by British troops the power of France could not subdue it in less time than Edward the 3rd reduced Calais.[24] Indeed, some of the French soldiers seemed dissatisfied with the bargain. The Royals took possession of the gate and drawbridge and the 71st on the left, while the garrison was marching out as prisoners-of-war. One

9

man had a large bass fiddle; on coming to the march in a rage he flung it as far as he possibly could. This was on the 18th. They marched to Fort Dan Haak, piled arms and embarked for England as prisoners-of-war. Our loss was Lieut Donald McLean, 1 drummer and 8 rank and file killed; Captain Wilson, Lieut Jackson and Mackenzie, 7 Sergeants and 81 rank and file wounded; 6 rank and file missing. On entering the town the destruction committed by our shells was horrible. Whole houses were one heap of ruins while the streets were in many places impassable owing to the falling houses and in some places the shells, having buried themselves in their descent and exploding, left chasms sufficient to bury a wagon. I heard an Englishman (who had been living there a number of years) say that the town would not recover the damage it had sustained in 50 years.

We remained but one night in Flushing, and then embarked for Antwerp, whither the bird had flown (that is the French fleet), but owing to the difficulty of navigating the river it took up more time than could be spared on such urgent business.[25] We were often snug on a sand bank until the next tide released us. The officers frequently got on a bank during the absence of the tide to fire at bottles. At length we got as close to Antwerp as was judged prudent; that is a respectful distance from the garrison and fleet.

But all our grand expedition may be said to terminate here, as the Army was detained so long in reducing Flushing. The enemy had time to march such a number of troops to the assistance of Antwerp, that it would have been but one remove from madness to have attempted a landing. In fact the whole coast seemed at night to be one mass of, or encampments of, troops. So after our gunboats had given them a few shells into the fleet, we came to the right about and relanded at Walcheren again.

Here we were sent to the different villages, but the air and stagnant water of this unwholesome though beautiful island proved to be the grave of many a British soldier, as the fever and ague[26] swept them off in great numbers. A slight idea may be formed of this unhealthy climate when on the 7th September the sick of the Army amounted to 10,948. Among the rest I made one, having caught the ague, and was sent home to England on the 30th September and landed at Harwich, from thence to Colchester, where I abode that winter in a wooden house.

Thus terminated in the conquest of a graveyard one of the finest, as well as one of the worst conducted armaments, that ever England sent from her shores. I believe the principal object was to lay hold of the French fleet then at Flushing. In attempting to do so I ask in the name of common sense what could bewitch the Earl of Chatham to land the Army on the island of Walcheren, and lay siege to Flushing, when he was aware that the fleet had escaped to Antwerp. One, or two of our 74s would have been sufficient to have given abundance of employment to the batteries [of the garrison at Flushing] while the Army, or at least the principal part, effected a landing and laid siege to Antwerp, then garrisoned with 1,500 men. The French fleet might, in all proba- bility, have been at anchor in the downs, nearly as soon as Flushing was in our possession. Again, when nothing more was to be gained, why was so fine an Army left to moulder away (or rather be destroyed) in so unhealthy a spot when such a reinforce- ment (nay a fourth of it) sent to Wellington would have prevented the tri-coloured flag floating on the walls of Almeida, Cuidad Rodrigo or Badajoz, which afterwards was the cause of so much bloodshed . . . Proposing an opinion on this disastrous expedition is rather a delicate concern. For as Burns says,

'The Best laid schemes of mice and men gang aft agley
And leave us nought but grief and pain for promised joy.'

But the Earl of Chatham's schemes were far from being well laid, and how could he expect success? Not by lying in bed to 10 or 11 o'clock in the day, when he ought to have been up and doing. There is no doubt, he might have filled some other situation with honour, but he was far from being competent in such an undertak- ing. Had he had the slightest knowledge of warfare, he would have acted very differently. Instead of driving the French into Flushing, he would have pushed on and taken possession of the different roads leading into the garrison, and by so doing would have prevented those in the interior from reinforcing it, and obliged them to surrender. It is more than likely thus circum- stanced that Flushing would not have stood one day's siege. But it was a mismanaged job altogether, and as is generally the case when failure takes place, blame is attached to every subordinate while the responsible person, being of rank, must by all means be exonerated.

Whether through ignorance or craft I cannot say, but on our landing[27] a halfpenny was as much value as a guinea. You could get 2 quarts of new milk for the halfpenny, and for a guinea no more. A button off the great coat with the eye smoothed down passed current for a shilling. Westcapelle was our Headquarters. Major Gordon sent his servant one morning for a change of a guinea; he returned in a little time, but what must have been the Major's surprise, when out of 21 shillings, 17 turned out to be soldiers' buttons. He immediately conjectured how this kind of coin came into circulation, and ordered a parade with loose greatcoats. For every large button missing he charged 1/- and for every small one 6d. Nor could they grumble, as they had only to refund the money they had received.

The effects of the climate on the Army was felt afterwards on the Peninsula[28] through the different campaigns.

Here we remained (that is the sick) through the winter of 1809. To each wooden room 6 men were told off, and frequently have I seen 5 out of the 6 in the shakes at the same time. As Spring approached the disorder began to abate, and to the credit of those who came forward at that time to relieve the sufferers the Quakers[29] stand in the foremost rank. To each man they made a present of 2 flannel shirts and 2 pair drawers, which was of the greatest comfort and utility in renovating our emaciated frames. This boon, so seasonable, shall while I have life be held in grateful remembrance.

Chapter Two

To War Again: The Battles of Busaco and Sabugal

In 1807 the Portuguese Council of Regency appealed to the British for assistance in driving out the French who had occupied their country. The situation in the Iberian Peninsula deteriorated even further in 1808, when Napoleon imposed his brother Joseph (then King of Sicily) upon the Spanish as their King, precipitating a rebellion involving the great majority of the Spanish people and the British government decided to act. A small expedition, commanded by Lieutenant General Sir Arthur Wellesley (hereafter Wellington), was sent to cooperate with the Portuguese and Spanish commanders, though, as this chapter reveals, the Portuguese Army had by then virtually disintegrated. The force reached Oporto on 28 July, 1808, having been refused a landing by the Spanish at Corunna. Almost at once its strength was considerably increased and a number of officers senior to Wellington also arrived, creating a thoroughly unsatisfactory command situation. Nevertheless, tactical control remained in Wellington's hands and within a month he had inflicted a heavy defeat on General Junot at Vimiero, so heavy that Junot offered to withdraw from Portugal. This withdrawal was negotiated in the Convention of Cintra whereby it was agreed that the French should be transferred to La Rochelle in British ships, a decision that was very ill-received in London and led to the withdrawal of all the senior officers involved, including Wellington.

In October the British government decided to commit a force of some 30,000 infantry and 5,000 cavalry to Northern Spain under the command of Sir John Moore, who was already in Portugal. The bulk of the force was to come from the army in

Portugal with a further 10,000 men arriving at Corunna from England. The two elements would meet in the general area of the River Ebro and conduct operations against the French in conjunction with the Spanish. However, the rout of the Spanish by the French and the fall of Madrid, together with a total lack of cooperation from the Spanish Junta and its senior officers, left Moore with no option but to withdraw his force from the country, for he realized that he had to face the whole strength of the French Army, commanded by Napoleon himself. With great skill and determination, harassed by Marshal Soult and plagued by appalling weather conditions, he withdrew up the difficult route to Corunna where, despite his losses en route and the desperate state of his starving and weary troops, he defeated Soult in battle, though at the cost of his own life. What was left of his army escaped and Napoleon's own strategy was in disarray, thanks to the delay that Moore had imposed upon him.

In 1810 the French executed their most determined campaign to date to drive the British out of Portugal. Marshal Masséna, with some 70,000 men, seized the border fortresses of Almeida and Ciudad Rodrigo and headed for Lisbon. Meanwhile Wellington, who had been recalled to the Peninsula in 1809, was waiting for him at Busaco, a natural defensive position, and inflicted a severe defeat on him.

Since his return, Wellington had been preparing an impregnable defensive triple line of forts north of Lisbon, the work of Colonel Richard Fletcher RE and seventeen sapper officers, supervising the efforts of some 10,000 local labourers. It was a masterpiece, taking full advantage of every natural feature and obstacle. It was to those defences, known as the Lines of Torres Vedras, that Wellington now withdrew his army, as Douglas describes. He had followed a scorched earth policy along the route that the French had been bound to follow and Masséna was now faced with an impotent siege situation and an army facing death from starvation. In March, 1811, having lost 25,000 men, he withdrew into Spain, a withdrawal that marked a turning point in the war.

*   *   *

The Battalion, having returned home, were quartered in Malden, Essex. I used every means in my power to join them again, but contrary to my expectations, had to join the 4th Battalion until completely recovered. That was a blow I was not prepared for, and I think at that time that transportation[1] would have been nearly as acceptable. It is an old remark that sorrow seldom comes alone and in this case it proved correct. Having slept the night in the barracks I was seized with the ophthalmia, and hurried off to Danbury, at that time a depot for those tormented with this disorder. The 3rd Battalion was now to be filled up again. I made application and though far from well I had the satisfaction of being ordered to join. I must appeal to the feelings of the soldier, after an absence of some time occasioned by sickness to appreciate the joy he feels at again meeting his comrades, and the hearty welcome he receives can only be surpassed by the parental home.

Early in the Spring of 1810, being ready for service, we marched for Portsmouth to embark, as was currently reported, for Gibraltar, as that Garrison was threatened by Bonaparte. On embarking, a portion of women were allowed to accompany the Regiment, 6 to each company, but our female ranks[2] mustered a great many more than this complement, so that lots should be drawn as to who should go and who should return home. Those of the latter class were to be paid a certain rate of mile for themselves and children and furnished with a free passage if having to leave the country. A woman of our company, Mrs Clarke, having lost her lot, was ordered out of the ship (the *Francis and Harriot* of London) to proceed home. On going down the side of the ship, 'I wish,' said she, 'the bloody ship and all that's in it may go to the bottom.' That was her prayer, and her husband in the ship!

We had some rough weather on the passage, when two of our brigs happened to get foul of each other, and another vessel conveying part of the 9th Regiment was also separated from the main convoy. The gale at this time had abated but the swell continued, which rendered their situation none of the most enviable. The crews of each vessel were mixed pell-mell. The Holy Boys (or 9th)[3] carried off the contents of the caboose, leaving the officers of the 38th minus a dinner.

Arrival in Portugal and the March to Busaco
Instead of Gibraltar we landed at Black Horse Square, Lisbon, on the 30th March, 1810. The appearance of the City from the River[4] is delightful, but with the exception of the above square and a few streets, it is the filthiest city I believe in existence, as all sorts of nuisance gets leave to remain in the streets, such as dead cats, dogs and filth of every description until the rain comes which is their only scavenger and sweeps all into the Tagus. The scent

15

which the frying of fish sends forth from pans over charcoal fires at the different doors is not very agreeable to the stranger's nasal organ while the lazy beings stretched on stone benches, wrapped in shapeless cloaks, enjoying the heat, may be seen, suddenly raised into the heat of revenge upon their tormentors[5], who are not so light of foot as those of the black breed.

We occupied the convent of St Benito, where we were very comfortable for some time. Here my old Walcheren companion, the Ague paid me his farewell visit, after intruding on my hospitality for 7 months. Yet it was well to get rid of him on such easy terms. The warm climate and good wine contributed not a little to banish his trembling Majesty.

Early in July we marched for Thomar, a fine town on the Tagus, with a large convent on the hill which overlooks the town, where we were quartered with the 2nd Battalion 38th, Lieut Col Nugent, and the 9th commanded by Lieut Col Cameron[6], together with 3 new regiments of Portuguese[7], forming the 5th Division[8], under the command of Major Genl Sir James Leith.

To give us a relish for the field we were encamped for a short time at a place called Barka de Cades about 3 leagues from Thomar and returned again a few days before we marched to join the Army then falling back after the fall of Almeida[10], and concentrating their force on the lofty and rugged ridge of Saira de Busaco, we crossed the Mondego on a bridge of boats. After many marches and countermarches we arrived at the foot of the ridge which was no easy matter to ascend, being obliged to drag up the gun, shot and shell in places which would have given a goat something to do to keep its footing, but there is nothing too hard for perseverance. With great labour and fatigue the job was accomplished. In some places it took 200 men with drag ropes to one 9 pounder, while other parties were employed in carrying shot and shell, each man taking 2 rounds. On the 26th September, the men being nearly worn down with constant fatigue, grew careless, and not attending to a howitzer on the drag ropes, they let her too near the slope of the hill facing the enemy . . . losing her equilibrium, she became unmanageable, and away she started for the French lines. After getting the reins [i.e. gathering momentum] she went with speed that would have thrown steam in the background. The 1st rock she struck her carriage flew in every direction, and then the barrel bounding from rock to rock she soon found a bed more peaceable than with us. Having reached the summit of the ridge near to where a large pile of fagots and

16

other combustible matter was collected for the purpose of firing, as a signal to the army in case the enemy attempted the hill in the night, we were standing in close column and had the happiness of stretching our wearied limbs for a short time.

The Battle of Busaco

Every man was asleep in a few minutes. It is a fact undeniable, let a soldier be ever so hungry and weary, and in the most profound sleep, at the whisper of stand to arms the whole camp was ready for action in 5 minutes, for be it borne in mind that soldiers when convenient[11] the enemy lie down fully accoutred with Brown Bess[12] in his arms. The morning of the 27th September 1810 was ushered in by the pickets popping at each other. At first little notice was taken but the fire increasing rapidly we got under arms and marched to the support of the troops defending the centre. Most fortunate it was we did so for just as we reached the ground, which was very rugged, we were obliged to form sections and double quick, which brought us to the scratch in the nick of time, as the French here forced the hill and the Portuguese having given way were in the utmost confusion; had not our Brigade made their appearance, I might say at the moment the consequences might have proved fatal to the Army, as it would have been completely separated. A small opening between the rocks of level ground admitted of a few companies wheeling into line, while the enemy on either side from the rocks kept up a quick and destructive fire. From this point, all along the left of the ridge we were hotly engaged, but on this spot alone it seems curious that they should have selected it for the grand attack, and which was defended by the Portuguese.

The Brigade being left in front, brought the 9th just into action, as the ground would not admit of more than one regiment in front, the 38th supported the 9th while we inclined to the left to form on the face of the ridge ere we had got into line as no time was to be lost. The brave 9th showered in such a volley as made room for the bayonet and down the steep face of the hill they fled in confusion. We now became exposed to the fire of a battery erected on a hill covered with young pine, though considerably lower than the one we occupied, which did their own men as much damage as the British. As it would have been a useless waste of human life to follow the discomfited foe beyond the boundaries of the Lieree[13], we were now ordered to retire and leave them to meditate on a fresh plan of attack.

The remainder of the day passed off perfectly quiet, but towards the left the sport was still kept up. On retiring the battery alluded to did considerable execution. Major Gordon who commanded was mounted on a beautiful little Walcheren pony and a shell fell close to its head which made the animal start and nearly upset the Major. 'Damn you,' cries he in a rage, 'I'll teach you to start at French balls,' and was in the act of plunging his sword into the beast when a grenadier prevented him.

The cannonading was continued on both sides the whole day of the 27th. That night being on picket we were stationed about half way down the hill with double sentries close to a rivulet which separated the two armies. The day had been extremely warm and on so elevated a space water scarce, which caused many a longing glance at the brook. However, as night closed in the French sentinel made the first advance towards a refreshment by laying down his firelock and signing for drink. His example was soon followed and, meeting at the brook, we had a most delightful draught, shook hands and resumed our post, just in time, as Major Gordon was field officer[14] and a strict disciplinarian. Had he detected us in the act, in all probability we would have had the honour of being shot. This was a place where, if I lay down, a dead Frenchman was my fellow; nor could it be avoided, as they lay so thick on the spot where the picket was posted. Major Gordon, as I already observed, being a field officer and on going his rounds, he halted to look at a soldier of the 9th and a Frenchman both dead, with their bayonets transfixed through each other. Viewing them about a minute, he exclaimed, 'There they lie like two gamecocks'.

A little after daylight a trumpeter advanced with a flag of truce, and sounded a parley. He was met by a Sergeant, and a file of men unarmed, who met him half way. His errand proved to be for leave to bring a General Officer his baggage, that had sprained his leg in the hurry of jumping from the rocks and was taken prisoner on the 27th. On the morning of the 28th we were very busily engaged, looking for the wounded among the rocks and bushes, numbers of whom we found in an exhausted state, but might survive with proper care. The day passed off pretty quietly. The enemy found that there was but little chance in endeavouring to force us off the ridge. They commenced a flank attack to the right, which caused his Lordship[15] to abandon the hill on the night of the 29th a little before midnight, leaving parties to keep up the fire to cloak the retreat.

The weather was uncommonly fine, but nights were, as might be expected, cold. We were just on the point of scrambling down the mountain when a hogshead of rum was ordered to be staved, the General[16] looking on. A little would have been of the greatest service. 'Twas clear day ere we reached the foot of the hill, where stood a village crowded with sick and wounded, whom we were obliged to leave in the care of the enemy. We marched on that day hot and dusty, without water, leaving Coimbra on the right, and forded the Mondego, a little below the town. Here our old Colonel[17] joined us as Brigadier General.

'Twas really laughable to see the Portuguese soldiers, as they forded the river. In went the firelock and with a handful of sand would get a famous scrubbing, so ignorant they were as to the care of arms. I merely mention this that it may be seen what sort of troops we had to depend on. Yet these new raised Regiments proved in a short time what discipline is able to accomplish with proper officers. I recollect one Regiment which belonged to our division; commanded by Major Hill.[18] This was the 84 Cassadores[19] or light infantry. They were formed in Thomar late in 1810 and of all the collections that I ever witnessed to make soldiers of they exceeded. That regiment at Salamanca behaved equal to the bravest of the British and every other regiment. But be it remembered, they were officered by the British. As to the mode of enlisting or pressing men for service, I cannot exactly say but their manner of conducting recruits (if I may be allowed the expression) to the places assigned for their reception would be more than the gravity of a White Quaker would bear without a laugh. You must not expect to hear of a Sergeant conducting a party of men voluntarily enlisted as soldiers; but fancy for a moment a Gendarme, or more to the understanding of the generality of the British, a mounted policeman, with a rope fastened to the saddle and tail of the horse, and at a distance of 2 yards a man secured. In this manner have I seen as many as 20 or 30 on the string, moving on to the receiving depot, which was generally some old convent, where they were kept not on the best of fare until they consented to volunteer. They were then liberated, clothed and equipped.

The Portuguese women, in respect of economy, were far superior to the British, as they in general carried all their movables, that is their camp furniture, in a bundle on their heads, whereas ours had to call in the assistance of a donkey. These last

19

were numerous and, together with mules, kicked up such a noise through the night as often to disturb the whole camp; and often dangerous rows took place between the belligerent parties to the no small amusement of our wearied frames.

To this day when I look back on the retreat from Busaco, I still pity the unfortunate inhabitants plundered by both friends and enemies, but it is not possible for those unaccustomed to such sights to form the most distant idea of the distress of the inhabitants. If you could picture to yourselves a family hastily packing up the most valuable of their substance on one or more bullock carts, bidding no doubt a farewell to the spot of their birth; a spot in all probability, if they survived and returned, the naked walls alone pointed out the spot where joy and gladness reigned. Those carts, which are none of the quickest or safest conveyances are generally drawn by two bullocks. The cart is of the rudest construction, and I might venture to assert that since the first of the Braganzas[20] there has been no deviation from the original, so firmly are the Portuguese wedded to the customs and manners of their forefathers. Often on this retreat has it happened that urging the poor animals beyond their strength to avoid falling into the hands of the enemy, either the beasts give up, or the cart breaks down, and all is irrecoverably lost, while the unfortunate owners wander on destitute of all save the life which they had put into the hands of strangers.

We passed through the town of Condatia[21] which had been a depot of stores. 'Twas now a scene of confusion and destruction. Here were piles of shoes, ready to be fired with Mr Red Hackles[22] on horseback with a pistol in his hand, ready to send any barefoot soldier to his long home that dared to lift a pair, which might have been the saving of his life, or at least have prevented him from falling into the hands of the enemy. Outside the town a vast pile of ammunition in casks stood ready for the train[23] to be fired as well as a large quantity of biscuits in bags.

We encamped about 3 leagues from the town in a wood of large pines. About midnight the whole camp was in an uproar owing to the explosion having taken place, when every tree nay the ground trembled as if an earthquake had taken place. The following morning we proceeded on our march towards Leyria, as fine an inland town as I had met with in Portugal. Here the enemy were close at hand and the destruction of property both public and private was great. The channels of the streets actually ran with wine; the vessels containing the wine had been staved in rather than let the liquor fall into the hands of the enemy. A curious occurrence took place here. The Germans[24] being taken by the Provost in the wine cellar were suspended by the neck from an olive tree outside the town. The French, being close, cut them down, and strange to relate both recovered and, as might naturally be expected, joined the French ranks. I do not give the above as authentic, but it was currently believed to be fact.

We pushed on towards Rymeo, a beautiful village outside of which we halted. Our wood and water parties were despatched in quest of these indispensables to commence cooking. I had my comrade's canteen with my own full of fine water, with something in the haversack, when 5 subaltern officers sitting on the trunk of a felled pine asked me for one of the canteens. 'No gentlemen,' was the reply, 'You have servants of your own, and this is little enough for my comrades and I.' They looked at each other, and I confess I felt the injustice of my refusal, but did not amend my conduct by returning and offering them a beverage. It is a fact that in 19 cases out of 20 the subaltern officers were, in respect of food, worse off than the private soldier, as their rank prohibited them from partaking in, or looking for a little grub if it could be found; not that a good fellow, as he was termed, whose eyes were not always open, would be forgotten if any roughness was in the way.

On we went making for the chain of batteries which extended down this arm of the Peninsula, commonly called the lines of Torres Vedras.

The grand battery was within a few miles of the town of Soberal, the entrance to which, like most of the Portuguese towns, is rather more than ankle deep in mud. The weather, hitherto fine now became wet. The roads, if bad in fine weather, were now most miserable. Soberal is a fine town. On the left of the road stood a large row of stones for the accommodation of those who were not disposed to be mid-leg deep in mud, and on the troops coming up, 'twas laughable to see them struggling for these steps, though it was next to an impossibility to be more filthy than they were, when Captain Smith rode up and says, 'Go through it you featherbed sons of b-s'. A general laugh ensued, and I believe I was the only one to reply, 'Well if this be featherbed soldiering, I have done.'

We passed on and encamped in a beautiful field of grapes, but in the course of the night it commenced to rain with a gale of wind and we were awakened in the morning not by the bugle, but the water running over us in the trench as we lay between the bushes. To attempt a description of our misery would be a task too hard for my old pen, and can only be conceived by those who have been similarly situated. All the resource we had was to stand upright and let the water run off as well as possible. The packing up of the knapsack was no easy job, still it was laughable to see the water fly yards high every shake the old blanket would get. Every man was a walking fountain that day as the water kept running from the pack. After plodding through the fields for some hours we got stowed away in something like what Goldsmith says of Sweet Auburn[25], but to be over-nice in the choice of quarter was now out of the question, as anything that would ward off the pitiless storm was nothing short of a complete treat. Indeed, it was mortally impossible for any human being to remain in the open fields. The following day we were ordered to a village said to be but 3 leagues distant, and as the mules that carried the spare ammunition had given up, the Col thought it a pity to let it be lost. Accordingly to meet his wishes (as he gave no pre-emptory orders) we were served out with a little more ballast in the shape of 20 rounds per man, making in all 80.

Roads or highways were now out of the question, and we proceeded with guides across the country, which with the quantity of rain that had fallen, together with bullocks, baggage, guns and followers of the army, the ground was so broken up that we were often mid-leg in mud, which required a good strong gaiter strap to preserve the shoe from being lost, but if that gave way, away went shoe and all. Our 3 league village being arrived at, it was something more than occupied, for it was literally crammed with Portuguese, so we had to go the right about and find a village for ourselves.

By this time I dare say more than of the Regiment were not complete with shoes. As for my own part I had lost the right foot shoe early in the day and had to plod through thick and thin in that state, and parade for outline picket in the evening. At length we reached a village which was occupied by the 71st Regiment of Foot, if I mistake not, just arrived from England with their new clothes. To contrast the two Regiments together, we poor, weatherbeaten, ragged, drenched barefoot beings and they so clean and regular, the remarks of an impartial judge at the time would have been curious. However, they had to turn out and let us in. Here as at Soberal large stones offered a clear retreat which the generality were disposed to avail themselves of while we stood laughing at such as were thrust into the mud and had to wade through this mire. Others, very soldier-like, marched through with as much composure as in a barracks square. Having got into a place of rest, I was stowed away with half a dozen men in a stable with some 12 or 14 mules, which was comfortable, having abundance of straw, and as the country people were driving their flocks through the town, in all the hurry and confusion we had nothing more than to stand at the door and choose either sheep or goat, lay hold of him and drag him in and pop him into the kettle. But if you went more honestly to work, you might have the pick of the flock for 4 or 5 guineas, as the owners imagined they might as well have that trifle as let the French have them for nothing. The poor creatures, their little all in front of them, and their little all diminishing daily, nay hourly. Yet clinging like the shipwrecked mariner to the last spar, they wandered on, cared for by none, plundered by all, till at length they sat down penniless to face a rigid winter in rear of the British batteries. Hear this statement, ye sons of Britain, and wonder. 'Tis easy for me to tell you this fact, and as easy for you to read it, and for a moment to be inclined to pity the unhappy sufferers. But how thankful ought the inhabitants of these favoured Isles to be, to the Author of all mercies, who has preserved them from the desolating hand of war.

Perinegra was the name of this village, and to this day I think the best white wine I ever made use of was here. The Regiment ere we started to the march had a pint per man, yet with this allowance I may fairly say the whole Regiment was intoxicated. It became a byword, when we got good wine afterwards to describe it as being equal to Perinegra.

*   *   *

At length we reached our ground and encamped under the grand battery above the town of Soberal, where we lay for the greatest part of the winter, pretty regularly rationed, but firing most miserably scarce, so much that it was rare to bring the meat to the boil. We used to eat it as thin as possible, and if you could bring the water to a good heat so as to take the red colour out of it all was right. But this kind of steam soup without salt was, in my opinion, not very nourishing and indeed many men got fluxed by it. Being so convenient to the shipping, which we could see in the harbour of Lisbon, we were regularly supplied with rations, and those Regiments who had come from Walcheren were ordered tents, which was very acceptable, but for the fact of being so small and so crowded. I have seen our hair frozen to the ground in the morning. Some time in January, the French, being tired of the blockade and provisions being not too plentiful, commenced a retreat of their own and fell back on Santarem and fortified their camp on the opposite side of the river. We broke up our camp and followed, but the desolating hand of sickness and starvation had rendered this fine spot, over which we had travelled a few months before, when it was stored with plenty, now a wilderness; not a mouthful of food for man or beast, while the wretched surviving inhabitants, though at all times none the cleanest, were now eaten up with vermin and dying of hunger. On the first day's march from Soberal I had the curiosity to number the victims of hunger and hardship that lay unburied along the road – men, horses, bullocks, etc – and they numbered 84; we being obliged in many cases to pass to leeward of the revolting remains of mortality. The stench was intolerable if we were to windward. The sight was shaking to a reflecting mind and prompted such an observer to break forth in that beautiful expression of a revered author, 'Oh thou Adam what hast thou done?'[26]

On this day's march a Corporal of our Company fell out and behind some bushes found a dead Frenchman. On examining his stock he found his cap full of Brazil tobacco. This was a valuable prize as at time we were very short of that commodity; so much so that we have often smoked wild mint and thyme. Tobacco was, I may say, the only thing which had the fascinating power of causing a soldier to part with his liquor for a few pipefuls. We arrived at Cortexo, which was our Headquarters for the remainder of the winter, and proceeded towards Santarem, which was in the possession of the enemy.

The Tagus being greatly swollen by reason of the late rains, the bridge leading into the town being well garnished with cannon, with redoubts and entrenchments in the rear, it was found advisable to let them enjoy dogs days rather than run the risk of losing a great number of men. It certainly would have cost a great many lives. Yet the attempt was proposed, but his Lordship rejected the proposal. We remained on the bank of the river viewing each other the greater part of the day, the rain descending in torrents, and then marched for Torres Vedras.

On the first day's march the roads were in a very bad state owing to the rain and being so cut up with the guns, baggage and bullocks, and in several places the enemy had to cut trenches across, both deep and wide, to impede our march. One place in particular the men were willing to avoid by going round a considerable way, but this was put a stop to by General Hay who sat on horseback by the side of the trench to see that every man kept his ranks as they plunged through the mud. These trenches in general were 8 feet wide and 6 deep, so that when nearly full it was no easy job to get clean through. On our Company coming up, the Officer in Command, willing to set an example, cries out as he made the plunge, 'Come men, dash,' no sooner said than in he floundered and was completely covered with red mud. Weary and dirty as we were, a general laugh ensued, in which the General could not help joining. The name of 'dash' that officer retained both in and out of the service to the day of his death.

Our Advance Resumed: the Battle of Sabugal
In Torres Vedras we were as comfortable as a stable would admit of for a few months. Early in March we started once more; the French having broke up from Santarem, leaving a sentinel on the bridge to observe the motions of the British. Masséna was rather too canny for his Lordship on this point, as the sentinel turned out to be French soldiers' clothes stuffed with straw. The pursuit commenced at all points. But this proved to be one of the hungriest marches we encountered during the war. Nor will it appear strange how this could happen when rightly understood. Say the troops marched 4 or 5 leagues each day at least, while the Commissariat mules with their provisions were not able to make 3 or 3½. Thus every day we were getting further away from our own rations, without the smallest hope of relief in our front; as the enemy left behind them a complete wilderness, and not content with depriving the unfortunate inhabitants of everything destroyable, committed the most wanton barbarities on the defenceless inhabitants as would be a disgrace to the original inhabitants of New Zealand. Nor is it fit to be related either in public or private. I am fully persuaded that a true born Frenchman would not be guilty of such enormities, as I have seen too much of their bravery, and bravery will not admit of such crimes.

We reached Rymeo, a fine village when we passed through it on the retreat from Busaco. It was now a miserable dirty den with very few surviving inhabitants. From thence to Leyria, which was one of the finest inland towns I had met with in Portugal, and in whose streets the wine ran in streams. 'Twas now nearly enveloped in flames, while the few inhabitants that remained were left

25

lying in their plundered houses, through wounds, sickness or hunger; being unable to escape the devouring element they perished in the flames. Before we entered the town, to the right of the road was a fine olive grove ... now nearly all destroyed, having been an encampment for cavalry. They could not have been gone many hours as their fires were still burning. Close to them lay a lad of about 12 years old, who appeared to have just expired. But such a sight as he presented will never leave my mind. The few rags he had on and every part of him appeared to be one moving mass of vermin. Passing through Leyria we kept to the main road leading to Coimbra, and kept on the greater part of the night, which was fine. Here you might observe men march along fast asleep, and at length tumble out of the ranks totally exhausted. Many a hearty prayer was offered up for the boys to halt, that we might get something,[27] either meat or wearables as our haversacks were completely empty, and the shirts shakers. The French in general carried fancy articles in the knapsack, such as white trousers, waistcoats, etc, and never without 30 or 40 rounds of ammunition, not that we often fell short of that commodity.

The enemy were driven past Coimbra with considerable loss, and to prevent our guns getting on had destroyed the road by cutting a trench across it both deep and wide, which impeded our march for some time, as in it lay a number of horses, mules, etc. houghed, and floundering about in a wretched condition. This was on the night of the 16th of March, 1811. We marched all night with fixed bayonets, as the guides were, or seemed to be, ignorant of our route. However, about 2 in the morning, we came in sight of fires, but whether friends or enemies was a question; but to our satisfaction it proved to be the British camp. We passed on between two hills, on the slopes of which the men rolled in their blankets and had the appearance of so many sheep. We kept the valley and proceeded to the front through the mire, to get a dry spot to lie down. But the French would not allow of our choosing a bed, and by way of sending us to rest let fly a 9 pounder at our advance, which said in language not to be mistaken, 'You are far enough'. The word 'halt' was given. The Col says, 'Take to your blankets men and make yourselves comfortable.' A general laugh then ensued. I am pretty confident that, dirty and hungry as we were, every man was asleep in ten minutes' time. When morning dawned a village was at hand, but the number of hungry soldiers who entered it in search of something to eat soon emptied it of the last head of Indian corn.

I think I shall say a little concerning Mrs Clarke, who put up so feeling a prayer for her husband on being ordered out of the ship when about to sail for Portugal. She, the following year, got smuggled out and joined the Regiment just before we advanced from Torres Vedras. Now being, like most of us, troubled with a pain in the haversack she made free with a fine piece of flesh from off one of the horses, carried it all night and cooked it in the morning.

The enemy were driven with considerable loss from Pombal, on the big guns beginning to play upon them. A man of our company noted as a profane swearer, and who had often been checked by his comrades for making use of such language, exclaimed, 'The devil is cleaning out his Barrack.' On another occasion, being severely reprimanded, his reply was 'I have nothing to do with myself. The Minister has charge of my soul, and the Doctor has charge of my body, so that I have no charge of myself whatever.' But for the credit of the Army it must be said, such characters were rare. Poor wretch, he fell afterwards at San Sebastian.

But to return to my story, on Patrick's Day[29] we were of great hopes that the enemy would engage in battle, but no, they moved off in the night and the pursuit continued. I seldom witnessed such enthusiasm among the troops, as they seemed one and all eager for a meeting, as if our Old Ireland's Patron saint had infused fresh spirits into their hungry frames.[30]

*   *   *

We arrived at the town of Miserella, a little above which the River Mondego takes its rise out of some rocks, and which I had the curiosity to visit. On the 2nd of April we ascended the mountain early in the morning, winding our way towards Sabugal. At night, after halting, we made ourselves as comfortable as the shelter of a stone fence was capable of, smoking our pipes and discoursing upon the expected brush with the enemy on the ensuing morning. Dixon, the gay fellow, as that was the name he went by, the same who upset the Major in the sea at Flushing, gives the quid[31] a turn and with a long squirt between his teeth of tobacco spittle cries, 'Who the Devil's father knows but they will change their disposition before morning,' meaning the French. Of course he meant their position. A general laugh ensued; not that he was a complete bull, for had he been a little skilled in letters he might with a little argument have turned the laugh on his side. We were formed in a chestnut grove on the side of the hill which prevented our seeing

27

the enemy, but were pretty well aware of their being convenient, as Col Nugent of the 38th rode up to Col Campbell, telling him that the French sentries and ours were not 20 yards asunder. After a halt of about 2 hours we were ordered to advance and attack the town, making the preparations usual on such occasions; viz, fix bayonets, prime and load. We advanced up the hill, from the summit of which we had a full view of the town and their position on the hill above it. As we advanced the enemy retired. A long and narrow bridge, leading to the town, might have been defended with success, at least for some time, but so great was their hurry that they abandoned it without firing a shot, leaving their kettles on their fires with their dinner nearly cooked. This you may imagine was no affront for as we double quick'd it over the bridge the fires were soon left bare, the men snatching the kettles off as they passed on. We dashed through the town and ascended the hill. This also might have been defended a length of time, but they fled leaving their tents standing. During this time the right was hotly engaged. Cannon and musketry were hammering away in great style. The first notice we had of how the play went on the right was the French retreating in the utmost confusion, while there we stood idle spectators (except a few 9 pounders), letting them pass with all the plunder of Portugal. There never was in my opinion so fine an opportunity lost as this. It is my firm belief that had we been allowed to have attacked the enemy at that time the army of Masséna would have been easily annihilated. General Hay rode up in a rage to General Dunlop[32], who commanded the Division, and demanded why he did not attack the enemy. His reply was, 'I am waiting for a guide.' 'There's the enemy, there's your guide,' exclaimed Hay. He then wanted his own Brigade to lead the attack, but 'No'; on which sheathing his sword with madness, he exclaimed in front of the Division, 'I shall report your cowardice to Lord Wellington this night,' and I believe he was as good as his word, as the General went off to England in a few days and did not make his appearance for several months.

The action, however, ended with honour for the British, but had the advantage been laid hold of that offered that day's work would have been one of the brightest laurels in the wreath that envelops the brow of Wellington.

A Dearth of provisions
A very heavy rain now fell and the firing ceased. Yet the cavalry followed them up the hills of Rendo, making some prisoners.

Chapter Three

Fuentes de Oñoro, Badajoz and Salamanca

Masséna's strategic withdrawal into Spain left the French with only a single foothold in Portugal – the small fortress town of Almeida. On 11 April, 1811, Wellington established a blockade of the garrison consisting of the 5th and 6th Divisions and a brigade of Portuguese militia under the overall command of Major General Denis Pack. Masséna, who had by now established his headquarters at Ciudad Rodrigo, was determined to relieve the garrison and advanced on Almeida with some 48,000 men. On learning of his approach, Wellington, with a much smaller force, had taken up a covering position around the village of Fuentes de Oñoro. After a fierce battle, which raged over several days and during which the village changed hands twice, the superior fighting qualities of Wellington's troops proved too much for Masséna who withdrew on 7 May – the defeat leading to his replacement in command by Marshal Marmont.

Even as the battle was being fought, Wellington had been driven to reduce the strength of the blockade in order to improve his general deployment. Although the French garrison showed plenty of spirit and resolve, after the disaster of Fuentes de Oñoro it was clear that they had no option but to escape from Almeida as best they might. Having blown up the magazine, as Douglas describes, they filtered through the sleeping picquets of the 6th Division and got away. Wellington was furious and never gave the divisional commander, Major General Alexander Campbell, another command.

Meanwhile in the south Beresford had invested Badajoz on 4 May but was forced to raise the siege by the return of Soult to the area in some strength. Having defeated Soult at Albuera on 16 May, Beresford returned to Badajoz and renewed the seige on 25 May only to learn on 12 June that Marmont was on his way to join Soult, so once again the seige was raised. Wellington decided to move north to invest Ciudad Rodrigo, which fell in January, 1812. Then, as soon as the flooding of the northern rivers made a French invasion of northern Portugal impracticable, he marched south again and re-opened the siege of Badajoz, which he entered on 7 April. Douglas describes the sheer horror of the ensuing rape of the city.

With both Ciudad Rodrigo and Badajoz in his hands, Wellington now controlled the northern and southern approaches from Spain into Portugal.

With his army numbering about 56,000 men, Wellington marched north again on 13 June and entered Salamanca on the 17th. Marmont, now reinforced, resumed the offensive but was crushingly defeated by Wellington at Salamanca on 22 July. He was severely wounded in the battle and replaced by Marshal Clausel.

With northern Spain in his hands, Wellington pursued the French through Valladolid to Madrid, where King Joseph Bonaparte had fled, leaving the city open for Wellington's entry of the 12 August. Leaving two divisions in Madrid, Wellington turned north again with four divisions to set siege to Burgos.

*   *   *

At length the enemy made an attempt to relieve the town, which drew on the battle of Fuentes D'Onor[1], on the banks of the River Coa, where here is the boundary of Spain and Portugal. We had been marching and counter-marching between Aspego, Collegno and little Almeida, which last-mentioned village is the first to be met with on this route into Spain. On the 5th of May we lined the Portuguese side of the river in extended order, as the Spanish side was very steep and rugged. It would have been no easy task to have forced our position on this point, so they ie the French drew on their left to Fuentes and thus commenced the battle.

Fuentes de Oñoro
The bridge leading over the Coa here was covered with our 9 pounder, close to which I and a man of the name of Teal were posted. (He had been Corporal, and on the march from Torres Vedras had affronted me, but it was out of my power to resent it

32

at the time.) However, we were in a hungry state for some days, and that morning had received 4 oz of rice. Some endeavoured to cook it in their mess tins, while others ate it as it was. Captain Beard recommended this later process, and to drink plenty of water; and then it would swell in the belly. However, there was no time for much nicety as the enemy made their appearance on the hill above us, and the musket balls began to fly about pretty thick. A man of the name of Edward Hughes, taking his allowance in his hand, and looking at it some time said, 'Well if I can live with you I can live without you.' So saying he strewed it on the bank of a river for a crop the following year. Another man exclaimed, 'Oh if I was but a horse, that I might eat grass.' Teal got reduced in rank, and now being on equal footing with him, and not in the best of humours from hunger, I thought of his behaviour. I says, 'Teal do you remember the march from Torres Vedras?; 'I do . . . what of that?' 'Why then, if you're a man stand out and box me.' Folding his arms, and staring at me, he says, 'You beat all the men I ever saw pointing with your fingers. There's the bloody French coming down the hill and you want me to go and box.' It certainly was rather a ticklish place for boxing, as the balls were whizzing among the trees, at no measured time.

The enemy drew off to the left. We joined the Division and took up our position on the heights above the river, leaving the flank companies to skirmish, which was kept up with great spirit during the day. The French having got a sound drubbing on our right, gave up all hope of overcoming the garrison, and retreated, leaving them to shift for themselves.

Nothing of consequence took place on the left as the main push was on the right, except skirmishing, which was kept up with occasional fire from big guns during the day. Indeed, it would have been next to madness to have attempted to force our position and I dare say they were pretty well convinced of that. It is really wonderful to hear the grumbling that goes on if men hear other parts of the army engaged while they are kept standing idle.

The day after the action General Hay gave us a treat by allowing us to take off our accoutrements and clothes for the purpose of de-lousing as the weather was uncommonly warm; and not having had our clothes off for many days and nights, we were pretty well stocked with the grey horse. The general, taking off his shirt and twining it exclaimed, 'I'll put them a day's march in the rear.' 'Twas a regular and standing order that no man was to be seen de-lousing himself within 200 yards of the lines. Thus you see what attention was paid to the cleanliness and comfort of the men . . .

To see a Regiment of Spaniards[2] on the march was short of a treat. They would be extended some miles, while there may be seen a group huddled round a fire cooking and further on, in a convenient spot, another gang de-lousing each other, and some moving on in as many costumes as were worn by the different nations of Europe.[3]

The French garrison at Almeida, finding that all hope of relief was at an end, having the works mined ready to explode, left slow matches burning, while they stole out unperceived by the blockading force[4] and even made their way among the British troops as they lay snug in their blankets and gained a narrow pass called Barba de Pork, where the greater part escaped into Spain. 'Twas really a grand sight, on the first explosion taking place. We stood to our Arms and marched in the direction of the disaster, but too late. Yet the different mines, as they sprung, had an imposing effect in the darkness.

My old comrade Miller ate very hearty of what he thought was watercress, but turned out to be something poisonous, as he swelled up to such a degree that we had to brace him round with canteen straps to prevent his bursting. Off he went to Celirico[5] and we never saw him more.

In and Around Sabugal: The Battle

We now got into Spain. The armies kept hovering around Ciudad Rodrigo, which was now become the bone of contention. We were quartered for some time in Sabugal, which like all the frontier towns was completely eaten up between the two armies. From here we marched for Elvas, within 3 leagues of Badajoz. We marched by Guarda Castle O'Branco, and crossed the Tagus at Villa Vella. A rude bridge of Portuguese boats was thrown over here, none of the nicest but withal strong. Here Captain Glover of our Company was seating taking a drawing of the bridge. It was undoubtedly as fine a subject for the pencil as could be; the troops descending to the bridge, crossing it and winding up the hill on the opposite side in a special ascent while the broad deep Tagus ran majestically between two stupendous rocks, the rocks resembling a mountain cut perpendicular in two, after passing which it bent to the left and was lost to the view. We arrived at Niza and from thence to Portalegre and encamped for some time a short distance from the town. This was a fine town built on the side of a hill, and like most of the Portuguese towns its appearance at a distance is beautiful, but within is full of filth and excess.

We left here to retrace our steps as the enemy in our absence were making rather free, and accordingly recrossed the Tagus again and halted a few days in Castle O'Branco. This is a fine town and I might add clean! But this in a great measure may be accounted for by the fact that lying so high the filth ran off without any exertion on the part of the inhabitants. The Portuguese scavenger – that is, the heaviest rains – clears away all. We left Castle O'Branco (or White Castle) and were sent to different villages and towns on the frontier not too far distant from Ciudad Rodrigo. The greater part of the summer of 1811 we occupied the villages in, and round Sabugal, Le Jose and St Payo. Here we encamped in a wood, or forest, for a considerable time. The wild scenery of this land of nod was grand, branches and moss being so abundant that the men formed huts (it being their principal employment when off duty) as would have been a wonder to an American Indian. But as every rose has its thorn we were in danger of visits from the wolves.

The only duty we had to perform here independent of the regimental duties was the manning of 2 pickets, about 7 miles in the mountains, called St Martino, and Velverde. One beautiful night the sentry of our quarter guard, loitering on his post, had laid his firelock against a tree. He was walking about when lo and behold Mr Isgrim[6] paid him an unexpected visit, and got between him and the firelock, to reach which was now out of his power. The guard were all lying down round the remains of the fire. 'Twas now life or death with the poor fellow, as the wolf was closing on him, so setting up a yell he took to his heels. In an instant the guard was under arms. The Sergeant sung at the top of his voice, 'Stand to your Arms'. Well, I think such a turn out never was exceeded, the surprise of Cremona[7] excepted. Not a man had more than his trousers on, and a great many naked as a mug without a handle, with the exception of the accoutrements. All flew to their arms primed and loaded, and formed line ready for action, as we were sure the French were in the camp. In a little time, the true cause being made known, the word was passed to resume our huts. The joke now commenced and was carried on, I believe, the remainder of the night. The poor Sergeant was very nigh paying dear for his false alarm, as with some difficulty he got over being tried by a general Court Martial, with only the loss of his stripes.

The relieving of our pickets daily was no small fatigue. In this camp in rear of the quarter guard I erected a place for the colours and drums, with branches and different kinds of moss over the centre arch which contained the colours, the Sphinx[8] with the word 'Egypt' in white moss. After leaving this place the French destroyed the whole camp except this emblem of their defeat in Egypt. I had credit for 2 pickets[9] for my trouble, and considered myself well renumerated.

After the action at El Bodon,[10] we broke up our camp in the greatest hurry, falling back on Sabugal, which was Wellington's main ground for battle. I happened to be on the quarter guard and left in charge of the sick with two cars to proceed in that direction. Independent of the sick our quartermaster gave me in charge of 2 cars laden with his own private property, one of which was taken up with small casks of Dutch pipes and tobacco . . . He had lately arrived from Lisbon, and these were his principal commodities, brought for the men's comfort, and were sold at a pound of tobacco and its companion a pipe for 6/6. A ready market he found at this price, as little or nothing else could be had. We proceeded on as well as we possibly could do. We reached Le Jose. Here the Commissary[11] was in as great a hurry as we. Whatever could not be carried away was in the act of being destroyed. Into the store I popped and helped myself to a canteen of rum, some bread and beef. We now proceeded at as quick a pace as our poor bullocks could move, and were overtaken by General Hay, who inquired what cars these were, and then ordered that the Captain of the St Martin's picket should on his coming up cover the cars as long as he could without endangering the picket. These orders I delivered to Captain Donovan, on his arrival, and received this conciliatory answer: 'Make the best of your way, and if you find the cavalry getting too close leave the cars and save yourself.' We kept on with a good look out to the rear. The French at length made their appearance on the hill. We now concluded the game was up. At this moment the General commanding the Division rode up, halted and made inquiry concerning the cars, and our freight also. Finding that 2 of them contained private property, he ordered their contents to be thrown on the road, and to drive as quickly, or we would be prisoners in a few minutes. Having seen his orders carried into execution off he started. I was too great a friend of the pipe to suffer it to fall into the hands of the enemy without a struggle, as the pipe was always the friend in need. For let our hardships be ever so great, if we could muster a pipe of tobacco it proved a sovereign remedy, and though you might as well part with your blood as the ration liquor, yet it would be cheerfully done to obtain a few pipefuls. The casks of pipe and tobacco which were thrown off, as soon as the General disappeared I immediately replaced on the cars and on we drove. One cask got staved, the contents of which I distributed among the men, in the manner of prize money. Luckily, the enemy turned to the right to follow the 3rd Division, which left us to pursue our march unmolested. We reached the camp just as the wine was being served out, but ere it was divided the enemy appeared on the hill. Out went the wine, line was formed in a few minutes and we advanced to give them battle. On seeing the line closing on them, to the right they went.

We continued to fall back on Sabugal whither I bent my course all night and at daylight was within a few miles of the town. In my account of the journey to the quartermaster, I did not omit to mention how I had preserved his property against all hazards and got rewarded with 3 dollars, some pipes and tobacco. We were now sent to different villages for the better accommodation, quarters and rations.

The Horrors of Badajoz
The French retired, for want of food, into Spain and left Ciudad Rodrigo to its fate, thinking no doubt that this nest of hornets could not be soon, or so easily subdued. Nothing of importance took place until January 1812 when Ciudad Rodrigo[12] was besieged and taken by storm on the night of the 19th. After the breaches had been sufficiently repaired the army was put in motion for Badajoz. The trenches[13] were opened in March, when we reached Elvas and proceeded to the front to cover the siege. The breaches were found practicable[14] and we were ordered to rejoin the besieging force. All things being in readiness, on the night of the 6th of April Badajoz was doomed, and with it many a British soldier to destruction. We and the 9th formed Wellington's guard that night, and so lost our share of the glory in the fall of that fortress. The fire balls thrown into the ditches showed the advancing columns so clearly to the latent enemy that death or mortal wounds succeeded every round. Yet death in all its terrors was unable to quench the courage of the British soldier. Amidst the storm of bullets and missiles of death which were hurled on them, they stood braving the tempest which no human power could quell. Unable to enter, disdaining to retire, at length

the feint attack of a part of our division succeeded so well that Sir James Leith[15] turned it into a real one and entered the town, while the assault of the castle succeeded likewise and Badajoz was won.

At daylight we were ordered into the town. The sight, even to a soldier, was horrible. The instruments of death had been successfully applied on both sides; fragments of men torn to atoms met your view in every direction. The bridge leading to the main guard or entrance had been sprung[16] and our poor fellows found their mistake in the dark, tumbled in and were irrevocably lost, numbers of whom were floating. We piled arms in the main square. To attempt anything in the hope of a description of the scene that was going on would be a task not easily performed, and even could it be delineated no one (unless an eye-witness) would credit the tale. But rather than leave you altogether in the dark I shall relate a few passages. Fancy so many thousand soldiers let loose, unrestrained by any authority, mad after such slaughter, and I might say doubly so with brandy and rum. The excesses committed were horrible, nor could it be avoided, as any officer who would recall them to a sense of their duty ran the hazard of his life. An officer of the 30th Regiment lost his life in attempting to save a young woman from violation. But the principal scene of drunkenness took place in the bread and rum-store, which appeared to be a vault. Here the soldiers of all regiments were making themselves at home, sitting on the bent baskets which contained the biscuit. These baskets were something in shape like the baskets which carpenters carry their tools in. They were roaring and singing while others were employed in drawing up rum in casks from an underground store. Those below not being too well versed in slinging them dropped them when the casks were perhaps within a few feet of the surface; down they went and got staved. In this manner the floor of the vault became a sea of wine, and those who went down perfectly sober got drunk without drinking. A man of our company, named Brown, went down to send up some rum, but never returned; not that he alone was lost here, but many others. It was conjectured that they were stifled as they were never heard of more.

Our Adjutant, wishing to put a stop to this picnic, comes in, and in an authoritative tone demanded what they were doing in His Majesty's stores. One of the 95th, seizing his rifle[17], demanded to know what division he was Provost of.

Upon reflecting on this interrogation, he thought fit to be off

38

and ran for it, when just as he cleared the door a ball from the rifle told through the door post. In the streets the scene was at times laughable; here a fine fire blazing, while every tot[18] was in requisition. Up comes a soldier with his bayonet fixed and as much bacon and salt fish on it as it could skewer; when all goes into the fire, and down he sits beside the fire helping himself, and as many as chose to sliced a cut of the bacon. Large pots of honey stood in other places, while the drunken rascals could not let a swallow fly past without a dozen balls being fired after it. As to the bells of the steeples of the churches, they were in constant chime.[19]

I was selected by the colonel to go round to the mean break[20] and order the servants to bring in the horses. Such a sense of destruction as was here presented to the view baffles description. The very rungs (or steps of the ladders) by which the troops descended into the ditch were literally shot to atoms with musket balls, while underneath the dead and dying lay in heaps; some calling for a drink for God's sake while their drunken comrades were selling their booty without taking the least notice.

After returning I was ordered to get as many sober men as I could (which was not an easy task to be performed, as I think there was not one in the Regiment) and enter without distinction[21] and throw every bed I could meet with through the window into the street; while another party was appointed to carry them away for the use of the wounded. I shall not easily forget the first house I entered. On the ground floor I was met by the man (or owner) of the house. I suppose he was the only inhabitant I met with, and was now determined to have a puff of the pipe. A pipe I had but no tobacco, so pulling my steamer I asked the man to let me have a pipeful. He handed me his long brass box, out of which I filled the cutchembo.[22] I returned the box with thanks. He seemed for a moment amazed, and taking it out of my hand he burst into tears. I was unable to grant him redress for the work of destruction that was going on in the upper apartments, so lit my pipe while his rooms were knee deep in feathers.

A fine young man named Geo Darling was parading for guard in the evening. One of his comrades, not being properly recovered for drunkenness, fired his piece and Darling was numbered with the dead. We marched to camp on the morning of the 8th when the unfortunate man received the benefit of a court martial in the shape of 800 lashes. Here we had abundance of rations served out, and marched to stop the enemy's career who, taking advantage of our absence, had penetrated as far as Castle O'Branco, but hearing of the fate of Badajoz, fell back.

Salamanca
Nothing much happened on the march. We passed the Tagus once more and followed them up to Salamanca, in which place they had converted an old convent into a garrison. During our siege of this inconsiderable but difficult place the French Army were encamped a few miles from the town on the verge of a fine plain. Being on picket one day with part of the 38th Regiment, amusing ourselves, as the day was fine, with passing our remarks and conjectures, as to the result of our being so convenient to each other, up gallops his Lordship[24] with a few of his staff. Taking out his telescope he viewed their lines for a few minutes. Then, rolling himself in a boat cloak, he lay down on the ground and was soon asleep. The glass he handed to an Aide-de-Camp, telling him to have a look out and if he observed any movement to let him know. He had not lain more than half-an-hour when the Aide-de-Camp shook him soundly. Starting up and rubbing his eyes Wellington seizes the tube and views them a short time. 'Yes, they'll be off tonight,' he exclaimed. So, mounting his horse, off he went. He had scarcely got clear of the picket when a Pizzano, mounted on a fine smart little pony, came in front of our post cutting a great many antic manoeuvres. Sometimes he approached us at full gallop, flourishing his sword, reined about, and dashed in like manner at the French. These pranks he played several times and I dare say the French were as much amused as we were. At length, dismounting and taking hold of his old spring garda[25] he falls on one knee, fires and kills one of the French sentries. Mounting his charger, off he went, closely followed by several of their pickets, to no purpose, though several shots were fired at him.

True enough, the enemy retreated that night. The garrison in Salamanca being reduced[26] the French crossed the Tormes at Toro, breaking down the bridge. His Lordship did not think it proper to disturb them, but on the night of the 17th of July the French turned around on their pursuers, re-crossed the Tormes at Toro and drove in our own pickets. We got under arms about 10 at night. We were encamped at Nave del Reev, lying in the fields at night and going into quarters by day to shun the burning heat of the sun. We continued to retire until daylight, when we were ordered back to check the advance of the enemy, who were considerably outflanking some of our Division, putting their guns and baggage in danger. We advanced about a league when we came in full view of the enemy, and formed line for action with the usual examination of arms; not looking for burnished pieces, but blew down the barrel to see if the touchhole was clear, flints fast and all's well.

Our position retarded their progress for some time, until they had examined our strength. We retired again and halted on the side of a gentle declivity with a small rivulet in front and formed line, from line into square, for the purpose of keeping their cavalry in due bounds. Our squares were scarcely formed when Arthur[27] and all his staff came galloping down the hill, his head going like a weather cock while the French 9 pounders whizzed about fiercely. We could see, by the clouds of dust, the march of the enemy, when just in our front a French officer rode to the top of the hill which his Lordship had just descended, and fired a pistol. We were pretty well aware of the signal, for in the space of 5 minutes 7 artillery pieces opened fire upon us. 'Twas lucky that Leith had deployed us into line so that the round shot could not do the execution, which it would have done had they caught us in square. The first gun shot told near the colours, which carried away a poor fellow's leg and his boot flew into the air. The adjutant says, 'There's one man down'. After remaining about half an hour under this fire without returning the compliment, the guns ceased, and on came the cavalry. Each regiment now formed into square double quick. The horse of a poor fellow of the 14th Light Dragoons had received a ball in the breast, and at each long step and short one the blood flew as if from a spiggot. He got the horse as far as our square where he lay down and died, while his master burst into tears. We made the man get inside the square until the enemy would make the charge. On came the cavalry, but the menacing appearance of the squares rather cooled their courage.

We were formed the same as at Waterloo, something like a chequer board, so that the fire of one square would not interfere with another. They very deliberately moved about but at rather an humble distance, and retired altogether. We now deployed, expecting the guns to open and were not disappointed. The object for which we halted being accomplished – viz to let the other Divisions of the Army get extricated with the guns and baggage – under this galling fire we went to the right about, retiring in ordinary time; their guns playing on us as long as a shot could reach us. We retired all that day in column of companies, wheeling distance apart, marching over every obstacle that came in our way, fields of wheat, vines, etc which, with the heat of the day, and no water, rendered this as fatiguing a day's march as ever I remember. At night, after halting, we were obliged to fight for our water, as the French were in possession of the village from whence we were to be supplied. This was soon accomplished, and to cook we went, and then to rest our wearied frames, to prepare us for a similar job in the morning.

On the 19th the enemy kept on our left flank, we in the same order – our companies at wheeling distance – marching over everything that came in their way, while the guns were not slack in taking all advantages that the ground would admit of and the cavalry sporting between the 2 armies. The 20th passed in like manner as the preceding day, both armies waiting for and taking every advantage. The 21st was spent manoeuvring, taking up positions and leaving them for others. How easy it may appear to some, changing positions, but be assured, it's not easily done.

As might be supposed, and often attended with great loss, the 21st passed much the same as the 20th. At night I think it was one of the most dismal imaginable. The thunder rolled in awful peals, the glare of the broad sheets of lightning, with the rain that fell in torrents, seemed as if the angry heavens were making their displeasure felt at the scene about to take place. The 5th (or Green Horse)[28] were lying on our right. The awfulness of the night caused numbers of their horses to break from their picketing and run through our ranks as we lay drenched to a skin but unwilling to rise lest we should lose our berth in the ranks and miss a comfortable nap. My comrade being on the Commissary guard had made off with some rum and biscuit; and stealing down the lines he found the Regiment and commenced to count the companies; but by some mischance he awoke a man who impersonated me and got my intended refreshment, which would have been of no small service.

A Resounding Victory

The morning of 22nd July 1812 was as fine as the preceding night was dismal. A little after sunrise the wood and water parties were paraded and marched off to set about cooking, as we had for a wonder some days' advance of rations, which caused a man to exclaim, 'Well, if I am killed today I will be in with the Commissary for once.' And killed he was. We had not been gone more than half-an-hour when the pickets began to pop at each other and so smartly that I climbed a tree to look into the valley to see how the play went. Scarcely was I mounted when the bugles called us in. The wood and water went to wreck while we double quicked it into the line, on with the accoutrements, fell in and moved to our right not far from the Arapiles (see p. 44).

About 9 in the morning his Lordship was talking with the Captain of our brigade of artillery[29]. If I mistook not Captain W. Smith, the French were in dense columns, skirting a wood. A great number of the enemy staff appearing, he was ordered to try if one of the long 9 prs would reach them. He elevated the piece and let fly. Every eye was on the lookout to see where the shot would take place, and it appeared to strike the ground a few paces in front of the group, so that they left that spot in quick time.

In our present position, his Lordship wished to find out where the enemy's guns were planted, and pitched upon the following stratagem. He ordered our regiment, being the first at hand, down the hill, to move towards the enemy that their guns might open upon us; and thus, by devoting a few to destruction, be the means of saving a great many. We fixed bayonets, loaded and down the hill we went, marching on towards the French lines. Our position, you may be assured, was none of the most enviable. The ground being thick studded with short brushwood, which rendered it very difficult to keep proper order, we were covered by some squadrons of the Greens[30] but when we came on a level with their guns, such a murderous fire was opened as surpasses description. Here we stood a knocking down without the most distant hope of returning the compliment. In my opinion there is no situation in which men can be placed so trying as to keep them exposed to a heavy fire and not be allowed the privilege of self-defence. In about half an hour we were ordered to retire, at which time the heath was in flames around us from the bursting of the shells. Thus having ascertained where their guns were planted, we joined the Division again.

The skirmishing now wore a serious aspect. As the advance began the cannonading increased with equal spirit on both sides. The able commanders opposed to each other were not backward in seizing on the least mistake committed by the other. Yet there is one thing I must not omit to mention. The British placed the most unbounded confidence in the skill, courage and coolness of Wellington, and I firmly believe they thought he could not err, and not now but always considered themselves sure of victory when led by him. And where troops are possessed of this belief in a Commander, there is no reluctance in obeying, but join the fight with an enthusiasm not to be overcome. The French, on the other hand, were as confident of Marmont[31], who had so often led them to victory, but here their opponents were British, which made a material difference when compared with Turks or even the boasted Austrians, and to strike the decisive blow alone was his greatest ambition, as well as his greatest error, but not waiting a few days for the reinforcements which he knew were at hand, and in all human probability would have turned the scale in his favour. But acting the part of Melas at Marengo[32], he lost both the field and his arm.

*   *   *

I cannot say, as I have heard some say, that they[33] were no more concerned going into action than a common field day, but I am fully persuaded that the man possessed of a belief that there is a God . . . will have a kind of terror over him for which he cannot account, owing to the reflection that the next moment he may be numbered with the dead. For its an awful thing to fall (particularly unprepared) into the hands of the living God. I am far, very far, from thinking, or wish it to be understood, that it is cowardice. No, but show me the man who knows he has an immortal soul, and advancing under the destructive fire of the enemy, but will in his inmost soul offer up the prayer of the publican[34]. To bear me out in this, let 20, 30 nay as many thousands as ever mixed in battle, be advancing to the deadly strife and not one word can be heard in all that number, but move on silent as the grave. I now ask the reason for this awful silence. The answer is this: each man is employed as he ought to be with his maker. But when the fire is opened all is forgotten save king and country.

*   *   *

The Arapiles are two hills of a conical form, one of which was occupied by our troops, the other by the enemy, and stood on our right. The enemy about, or between one and two o'clock, commenced extending their left to outflank us, on which Sir James Leith advanced our Division in double quick time to check them on that point. Down we lay on the slope of the hill for the purpose of letting the round shot pass over us as quickly as possible. In this position we loaded. The 2nd Brigade formed in our rear. The

44

3rd Brigade on coming down did not please Sir James. He marched them back under the whole fire in ordinary time and back again to make them do it in a soldier-like manner. The Brigade, on coming to its ground, the centre sub-division of the 15th Portuguese[35] was struck with a shot (I mean cannon shot) which did fearful execution. It scarcely left a man standing.

On the 2nd Brigade forming a man of the 44th was killed and lay for a few minutes, when a shell fell under him and exploding drove him into the air. His knapsack, coat, shirt body and all flew in every direction. A Dublin lad lying on my right looks up and exclaims with the greatest gravity, 'There's an inspection of necessaries.'

The Spaniards seemed to have a great curiosity in viewing the combat. You would really imagine that the town of Salamanca was emptied of its inhabitants. The hill to the rear of our lines was as densely crowded as the Butt in the Park[36] on a birthday, or the anniversary of Waterloo, which did not escape the observation of the French, who, being busy as they were, took time to spare them a few rounds, which had such an effect upon them that in a very short time neither man nor woman were to be seen.

General Leith rode up about two o'clock. The cannonading at this time was terrible. Addressing the Regiment he says, 'Royals,' on which we all sprang up. 'Lie down men,' said he, though he sat on horse-back, exposed to the fire as calm as possible. 'This shall be a glorious day for Old England, if these bragadocian[37] rascals dare but stand their ground, we will display the point of the British bayonet, and where it is properly displayed no power is able to withstand it. All I request of you is to be steady and to obey your officers. Stand up men!' Then taking off his cocked hat and winding it around his head he gives the word 'March!' A few paces brought us to the crest of the hill when we became exposed to the fire of all the guns they could bring to bear on us. I think the advance of the British at Salamanca never was exceeded in any field. Captain Stewart of our company, stepping out of the ranks to the front, lays hold of Captain Glover and cries, 'Glover did you ever see such a line?' I am pretty confident that in the Regiments which composed our lines there was not a man 6 inches out of his place. The French seemed to be taken by surprise as the 1st Royal Dragoons, the 5th Green Horse and a Regiment of Heavy Germans[38] advanced with us on our right. Some of the Greens sung out, 'Now boys, lather them and we'll shave them.' As we approached the enemy their skirmishers retired, followed by ours and the Portuguese to within a few yards of their lines for seeing the British advancing through the tempest of balls, they[39] kept advancing in like manner to within a few yards of the enemy's pieces, crying out 'Fogo ma felias' or 'away my sons'. At this moment a French officer mounted on a white horse seemed to be very busy endeavouring to keep his men to their work, when a Corporal of the name of Joffrey and I got leave to try if he was ball proof; and running out a few yards in front kneeled down and fired together, but which of us struck him must still remain a mystery, but down he went. Poor Joffrey, while in the act of rising off his knee, received a ball in the breast which numbered him with the dead also.

It was with a good deal of difficulty that the skirmishers could be made to retire, that the lines might open their fire.[40] The enemy, as I before observed, seemed to be rather in confusion. The cavalry on our right was to them a puzzle. The enemy seemed to have formed parts of squares, and parts of lines, and before they could recover from their panic, our murderous fire opened, which swept all before it. Their first line we fairly ran over, and saw our men jumping over huge grenadiers, who lay down exhausted through heat and fatigue, unhurt, in the hope of escaping. Of course we left them uninjured, but they did not behave honourably, for as soon as they found us at a little distance they resumed the posture of the enemy and commenced to fire on our rear; but nearly the whole of them paid the price of their treachery with their lives.

The first line of the enemy being broken and falling back in confusion, the 2nd lined the side of a deep trench cut by the torrents of water which roll down from the hills near the village of Arapiles, and so deep and broad that it took a good spring to leap over it. Here the 2nd line kept up a heavy fire of musketry, which checked our centre for a few minutes, while our poor fellows fell fast. To remain long in this way was too much to be borne. The cheer was raised for the charge, a general bound was made at the chasm, and over we went like so many beagles, while the enemy gave way in confusion. The cavalry now came in for their share and cut them down in great number.

While this was occurring on the right, the 6th Division on our left was ordered to charge a hill crowned with cannon. The day was extremely warm. Our poor fellows, having to bear up against the united fire of cannon and musketry, had their ranks equally thinned ere they commenced to ascend the hill. So determined were the enemy to maintain this post that one brigade of our division was cut off. Fortunately, our work was settled on the right as the enemy were falling back in confusion. We brought up our right shoulder and flanked the hill, on which they gave way here also, abandoning their guns in disorder. 'Twas now near sunset, which appeared as red as sunset through the dense columns of smoke, while the cheers of the British advancing to the charge, and the peals of musketry which seemed to increase, was a scene so awfully grand that no pen could describe it. The 2nd Queens, the 11th and 61st were the Regiments which composed the Brigade I have mentioned . . . I never saw the British casualties so thick, while we passed on in pursuit, striving to avoid treading on the wounded, who were calling for a little water for God's sake, which was entirely out of our power to give; or in the more feeling accents of comrades they pleaded, 'Don't trample on us'.

A little after sunset the enemy was in full retreat, leaving us in possession of this well fought field. They were followed by the cavalry as long as light remained, but night saved the French army from destruction. A little before sunset a Portuguese soldier of our Division picked up an eagle[41] and brought it safe into the lines, to the astonishment of all as you would imagine that a sparrow could not escape between the two fires. This eagle was the subject of an account in a book of anecdotes a few years ago, when it was stated to have been captured by an officer of the British. The statement was false. It was taken as I have mentioned. It lay on the ground along with a number of the Regiment to which it belonged, having fallen by our fire, and was free to be picked up by anyone, but it was first discovered among the dead by the Portuguese soldier. But what became of it afterwards I cannot say, as I had other business to attend to. A poor hare as we were advancing sprung from his little house of refuge and made for the French lines. 'There's the hare, but where are the hounds?' cried Captain Stewart.

We halted for the night on the ground occupied by the enemy during the morning (or during the action) and sent out parties for water, having nearly 5 miles to travel before it was found, and then it was as green as the water you may have seen during the heat of summer in a stagnant pond. However, it went down with a fine relish. The only piece of plunder either I or my comrade had got happened to be a leg of mutton off a Frenchman's knapsack, which I put down in a kettle to boil, having made a fire of French firelocks. I was sitting on a stone watching the fire, musing over the day's work, when, rising up to look into the kettle, one of the pieces went off, the ball passing between my legs. This was the nearest visible escape I had, for if providence had not so ordered it that I rose at the instant, the contents would have been through my body. The breaking up of the ammunition wagons might be heard at a great distance as the men wanted firewood for cooking, and having regaled ourselves with whatever we could muster, lay down to rest our weary blackened frames, and in a sound sleep forgot the toils and dangers of the day. I was nearly omitting to mention that as I and my comrade were eating our mutton he got something indigestible under his tooth which proved to be a French ball which had lodged there during the action.

In Pursuit of the French

We were pretty early on our limbs, as the bugles called us to arms to pursue the foe. We started to the march, the day being uncommonly warm. I was ordered to bring up a sick man who had fallen out, unable to march. This was a task most distressing to non-commissioned officers. The man who fell out invariably left his firelock with the section to which he belonged. Thus he became a general burden, as every man had enough to do to carry his own equipment, and if he fell to the rear a mile 'twas no easy job to rejoin the ranks, owing in a great measure to the badness of the roads. I now got intermixed with the stragglers of the army and followed in the wake of the Division. The day was intensely hot and we were glad to find shelter in a wood. The ground fortunately proved to be marshy. Here you might observe the sick, parched creatures, kneeling down and scraping the mud away 'till they obtained a little water, then sucking it to the dregs. Hunger is bad, and not easily borne, but is nothing in comparison to thirst. From this place I proceeded with my charge as fast as possible, but this was not at too quick a pace, so that I was overtaken by an old schoolfellow of the 27th Regiment, with a hearty shake of the hand. 'Why,' said he, 'I was inquiring about you as the Regiment passed, and they told me you were killed yesterday.' 'Well Bob,' said I, 'You see it's a lie.' He having a little in the canteen, we drank to bygone days and distant friends. The heat of the day caused the stragglers to be very numerous. It would appear that every man was his own butcher, or at least killed his own meat, as the firing was so thick along the hills at the sheep. These in general were not so large as the Leicestershire breed, but their flesh uncommonly well flavoured, at least we hungry soldiers thought as much.

I reached the camp in time, close to the bridge of Alba De

Tormes, just as the wine was served out. Here we commenced getting our arms and accoutrements in order, to resume the pursuit. On the 24th we passed through the town and reached the heights of Peneranda. Here the French rearguard, consisting of three regiments, formed square against the cavalry, and if I may be allowed to form an opinion, defended themselves bravely, as the number of men and horses which lay on the spot told in language not to be mistaken they had done their duty; and the exactness of the squares, which was very visible by the sight of the Frenchmen and firelocks as they lay, no less a proof of the superior bravery of the British cavalry that had conquered them. We continued the pursuit but the weather, which was intensely warm, rendered our march very fatiguing. Some days marching through pine forests, where not a breath of air could reach us, while the black sand stirred into dense clouds with such a number of troops and the ever attendant followers of an Army, rendered it nearly suffocating. Our tents were very simple, soon pitched and as easily packed up. They (that is, each tent) consisted of 2 blankets, two firelocks and 4 bayonets. At each corner of the blanket a hole was worked similar to a buttonhole, and in the centre another. A firelock stood at each end, to serve as poles. The bayonet of these firelocks passed through the corner holes of both blankets, a ramrod secured the top, and a bayonet at each end fastened in the ground completed our house. These tents certainly were a shade from the scorching rays of the sun, yet the heat inside was intolerable.

We reached a mountain from whose summit we had a first though distant view of Madrid. On the right of the road near the top stands a monument erected to one of the Ferdinands.[42] We descended into the plain, which was large, and were lain down to rest when by some accident the long dry grass with which it was clothed caught fire, and, a breeze springing up at the time, the fire ran along with the rapidity of gunpowder, while clouds of insects, flying to escape, though quick on the wing, perished. The men were in as great haste to protect their ammunition, several pouches of which were blown up.

Within a short distance of Madrid, we encamped in something like a nobleman's demesne, where we had precious sport, after hares and rabbits; very few of which, being started made their escape. The underwood being thick and the men in every direction, if they escaped from one party they were sure to be captured by another.

Into Madrid and on to Burgos

On the 14th August we entered Madrid. I might have said it was our triumph as it exceeded all the exhibitions perhaps even witnessed by a British Army. The streets were so crowded that the troops could only with difficulty move on, while the cheers and vivas of the multitude were deafening; the windows crowded with females waving white handkerchiefs and drapery (if I may so call velvet) of the richest dyes hung suspended from the balconies, in many of which huge wax candles were burning in massive silver candlesticks. Our company picked up a half-madman, which gave us no small amusement, and served to keep off the mob. At parting he offered me some money, which being refused, he seemed highly affronted and threw it away.

With some difficulty we got through the city and encamped close to the outer wall of a fort called La China, which was itself weak but the works with which it was surrounded would have cost some blood before it would have fallen. It was garrisoned to 2000 men, and it appeared to be a depot of stores. They surrendered as prisoners of war, without firing a shot. This place appeared to be the residence of some nobleman, but the French turned it into a garrison. It contained an immense quantity of warlike stores, for equipping an army. My comrade being on guard there, the day after its surrender, came to the outer wall about midnight, and giving the concerted signal, which was instantly obeyed, threw down about a bushel of tobacco, with half a dozen good linen shirts and some shoes, which was no affront.

In the course of 2 days we marched again, keeping clear of the city, and got on the road to Escurial, a palace[43] built by Philip in honour of St Lawrence, a Saint that suffered martyrdom on an instrument in the form of a gridiron, at least it is so said. Be this as it may, it is an immense pile of building, and must have cost a good round sum. The village of Escurial is but small. On each side, as you enter from Madrid, you find a stout round wall loop-holed for the purpose of preventing surprise by the guerrillas. The Palace furnished abundance of fine quarters for the whole of the British and Portuguese troops, and to spare. I dare say it is one of the largest buildings (at least of the kind) in Europe. Some of the apartments were elegantly furnished, though I believe they were minus a few of their fine paintings in the morning.

From here we marched by way of Segovia and Arevalo, for Burgos. The harvest was now in its prime. Wheat, grapes, etc were more than abundant. In Arevalo, we started to grind the wheat, and succeeded amazingly well. The process was very simple. Large flagstones were plentiful here. These served as the nether millstone, while a piece just as large as a man could conveniently work formed the upper one. It must not be expected that we produced meal of the best quality, but to men having good appetites, and the tenor of the Commissariat far in the rear, it was, you may depend upon it, not to be despised. There were a few coffee mills in the Regiment which were of infinite use and produced excellent meal. I certainly would, if going on service again (which is more likely I will not)[44] have a small coffee meal; one to each company would not be amiss, as I have seen and proved their utility. We reached Valladolid, which the enemy abandoned. This is a fine ancient town; the appearance of the buildings certainly point to the days of Columbus. From here we passed through a delightful country. At the time the grapes were in the height of perfection, and in the fields (or rather the plains) we were under the necessity of encamping. At all times we were as far removed from those tempting articles as possible, but in the instance it was out of their power to avoid our eating them.

Chapter Four

Burgos: The Siege is Raised and We Retreat

By the end of August, 1812, Clausel had restored his army to its former effectiveness. However, as Wellington advanced with his four divisions from Madrid, Clausel fell back through Burgos, leaving the fortress to face Wellington's siege. It was now mid-September. Burgos, which was a very strong fortress and well garrisoned, proved too tough a nut for Wellington to crack, for he lacked adequate siege artillery.

Learning that Masséna, who had been restored to favour by Napoleon and now had command of all the French forces in the north of the Peninsula, had replaced Clausel with Souham and ordered the latter, who he had reinforced with 12,000 fresh troops, to relieve Burgos, Wellington raised the siege on 15 October. He began to retreat towards the River Douro, sending Hill down the valley of the Tagus. The two forces met on 8 November and took up positions on the River Tormes. Meanwhile, Souham had been joined by Soult, who now outflanked the British by crossing the upper reaches of the river, forcing Wellington to retreat yet again. By 17 December his army was behind the Portuguese frontier and he went into winter quarters.

*   *   *

We reached Burgos, and marched to the front, to cover the siege of the Castle.[1] Our rations were very good and pretty regular. I think the Spaniards, particularly round Burgos and Biscay, make the best bread in the world. I am much of the opinion they put a quantity of honey in it, and that article is plentiful here.

During the siege of this inconsiderable place, which was prolonged for want of material to an unusual length, and finally given up as a bad job[2], often have I had to go out to gather a few brambles, without shoe or stocking, for the purpose of making a light that I might be enabled to make a state of the company[3] the following day. The number of killed and wounded at Salamanca, with sickness, had so thinned our ranks that out of 6 Sergeants and as many Corporals, there was not one present with the company but myself.[4] Often at daylight, at which time the liquor was served out, I have drawn the company's allowance in two mess-tins, so that it may easily be conjectured we were not very strong; not more than 25 fit for duty in a company that, if all were present, numbered 100. My poor old tattered trousers and coat were no way improved by these excursions and in many cases it would have taken no mean judge to determine the original colour; perhaps a piece of stocking covered a few holes on one sleeve while a piece of biscuit bag covered the other. No matter what the colour was, if we were lucky enough to find a piece it found a place very soon on either coat or trousers. The last mentioned indispensables underwent many twinings[5]. I assure you we took more wear out of a pair of trousers than the most rigid economist of the present day.

The siege of the Castle continued, or rather languished, until the afternoon of the 21st October, when the enemy made their appearance in our front. Here we heard the old story, 'Stand to your arms.' Each man flew to his post and in the course of a few minutes formed line, primed and loaded, and advanced to give them battle. They appeared to be a mile in front, in fine order. We kept advancing and they moved to the right about and were soon out of sight in the mountains. It rarely happened that we were deficient of a joke. We were moving on, expecting to be engaged. One of our old privies had been closed up with earth, so that unless you were aware of the spot you would have been deceived. This was the case with a man of our Company named Ralph Moore. Poor Ralph, I suppose, was more intent on watching the enemy than where he set his foot. The slight covering giving way, in he foundered, and not without some difficulty got extricated, but the sight of Ralph and the perfume which he caused will never leave my memory. Of course he was no use in the ranks, and as to his arms and accoutrements they were completely spoiled, and, even had this not been the case, nobody could have stood the stench. Accordingly he fell out to get washed and join as best he could. Ralph was a true bred cockney, and used to say, 'I'd rather be hung in London than die a natural death in Portugal.'

We kept marching on all night, as we thought to the front, but lo and behold, when morning dawned we had the castle in our rear. It appeared we had made a complete circuit of the place, which led us to believe we were advancing. I think I was the last British soldier that passed it, just at dawn, having been left to bring up a drunken fellow of our light company who had been on the Provost guard and left sentinel over a skin of rum to see that the pizzano got justice[6], but not he alone, but two others who had fallen out unable to march were in the same predicament. Thus I had a precious charge, sometimes using flattery, other times threats, and all with little chance of joining the Division, as by this time I was well aware the enemy would be at our heels in a short time. Yet I had one consolation left, as the adjutant told me when I got charge of them that if I found the enemy close in the rear and could not get them away to abandon them and save myself.

A little after dawn we reached a village, which we were convinced the Division had passed through as it was mid-leg in mud. All was silent as the grave. By this time my precious charge began to come round a little, and seeing a light in a house we demanded admittance, until we threatened to fire, on which the door opened and a pizzano stood at the side of an oven hard at work. He begged to be excused from sharing with us, a request which we could not conscientiously comply with, so seized a 4 lb crusher and left him in no doubt pretty well satisfied with getting off so easily. On leaving the village we unfortunately took to the main road and so missed the Division. In the course of 2 hours we reached another village, and entered another house in search of some refreshment, but met with a stout dismissal. Anything in the shape of provisions had been carefully concealed. However, on looking up a chimney we found one of the finest chovieces[7] I ever saw. We quickly cooked this and it . . . made an excellent meal, but, being highly seasoned, rendered a drink very desirable. Accordingly, a search commenced and succeeded in discovering a cask concealed in the cellar, from which we slaked our thirst.

Scarcely had we concluded our repast when the village became crowded with Spanish soldiers, so eager to get on that the main road, though broad, could not contain them. I had now got into a pretty mess. Our Division had taken to the right, to be far off the line of march with the Spaniards, so I and my 3 drunken rascals

54

were the only redcoats that I could see on this line. The entrance to the village had a sharp turn which was nearly blocked up with baggage, and here the struggle for precedence was no light one. All order was lost, and everything in confusion and flight. The French guns opened on the mob, but such confusion as took place was really shameful to men willing themselves soldiers. The fields and gardens were in a few minutes one scene of flight, while I and my now 3 sober men could scarcely get extricated from among the fugitives. Had they possessed any spunk they might have defended the place for a considerable time, which would have enabled them to retreat in some kind of order. Finding it would not do to keep on with such light-footed gentry, I was rather puzzled as to what plan to adopt for the best. To remain with this rabble, 'twas a clear case I would very soon be in the hands of the French, and to stake off the main road either to right or left was all chance. Our Council of War ended rather abruptly, as the French cavalry rushed into the town and we were forced to take to the mountain on the right and scrambled up it in safety, giving them a few rounds at our leisure. On the summit we sat down to rest when, in the space of half an hour, when I got released of my charge, our presence met with the astonishment of all, as we were considered as taken prisoners, which would certainly have been the case had I not fortunately taken to the hill.

On this day's march we were not molested by the enemy. On the 23rd we marched again about 5 leagues and halted, as we supposed, for the day. But scarcely had we commenced to cook when we embarked on a second route, which extended for 3 leagues more[8], this being accomplished some time in the night. As the days began to shorten during this latter end of October, we of course expected to have a good nap after this march; but when about to lie down, a 3rd route awaited us for 2 leagues more. There was no use in grumbling and to the road we went, hungry, wet and weary. But ere it was complete, I think it was 2 in the morning. I have a statement by an author of the first class, speaking of the retreat from Burgos. He states, and indeed he quotes his Lordship's Orders in corroboration, 'that no army ever made shorter marches, nor one less harassed by the enemy.' In respect of the first part, I think it would not be easy to reconcile me to a belief that 30 miles, allowing 3 miles to the league, is a short march on an empty haversack. Of course we marched the lighter. And as to the 2nd part, we will explain, as we proceed, whether we were or were not harassed on the retreat. We lost a number of men this night, worn down with hunger and fatigue. They would throw themselves out of the ranks quite exhausted and in a short time were retracing their steps towards the frontiers of France. Our wood and water parties were directed to a village for these commodities, while the bullocks were slaughtered. But on their return, instead of water, every kempkettle was filled with wine, and no mistake. Others, instead of wood, had crocks of honey, and be assured, these commodities, though late, were not unwelcome.

I have seen a statement where it has been moved that the British Army acted more the part of bandit than soldier. But in the case I have just mentioned, show me the man, nay Father Mathew[9] himself, similarly situated. I question much if the pledge would not be trespassed on. For be assured that a drink of cold water, though delicious at times, is no great comfort to a keen appetite, and especially to dream upon. As to the soldiers plundering the inhabitants, I give it my most decided contradiction. For be it remembered the Spaniards do not live in that settled way in which the British do, but in villages for greater security. And these were too well looked after to be plundered, we not being allowed to enter them but march past and find the best beds you could on the wet earth. I certainly say, where we could obtain a little wine or grub we would make no scruple on making it our own. And even at this remote period, it would require sound judgement to convince me, by so doing, of having broken the 8th Commandment[10], for it is said necessity has no law.

We made the best use of our time here as far as good wine and a sound sleep would go, though the latter was rather short; at dawn of day our surprise was none of the most agreeable, as the enemy were entering the camp. A great many were in no condition (at least good condition) to receive such early visitors, and uninvited. Very few minutes elapsed before we were in a condition to return the salutation. Col Campbell[11] I think was actually mad, seeing the state the men were in and the enemy at hand. He fairly jumped on them as they lay; but ere the day's march was concluded he assumed his temper, as not a man fell out on the march.

The Engagement at Placencia

'Twas night when we reached the River Carrion, the bridge over which was nearly blockaded with men, baggage, guns and every species of trumpery attendant on an army. We made our way with no small difficulty, and encamped for the night on the heights facing the bridge, with Placencia on the left. This is a beautiful town situated at the foot of a mountain. A dry canal ran nearly parallel with the river, to near the town. A dilapidated bridge over the canal led to a beautiful green, ere you reached the town, where a noble bridge crossed the river leading into it. The order had been sent to our Division to blow up the bridge on the evening of the 24th, instead of halting on the heights. But unfortunately the Dragoon who carried the order lost his way in the dark and did not reach the Division until 8 o'clock in the morning, by which time the bridge ought to have been destroyed. The accident was the sole cause of the disasters of the day. As soon as the order arrived, the Artificers and Miners[12] of the Division were ordered down, covered by our battalion and two squadrons of dragoons. But having, I dare say, 4 miles to march, the morning was pretty far advanced ere we arrived there, and to work they went on the bridge. We were formed on a delightful green close to the river which separated us from the town, in open column of companies, not expecting the enemy to be so convenient; and as proof of our ignorance of the enemy being in the vicinity, the shoemakers of the different companies[13] marched into town to procure leather for the repair of the men's shoes, and everything went on as in the most secure camp. By this time the enemy were moving down the hills which overlooked the town, keeping up a desultory fire, which was taken for the stragglers shooting pigs; when all in a hurry our leather merchants came running down the lines and spread the alarm of the enemy being in the town. Scarcely had they reached the column when some close firing took place on the bridge, and the enemy got possession of it. The Engineer Officer comes running to Col Campbell and says, 'Col Campbell, the bridge is taken. You are at liberty to act as you please with your Battalion.' Thus were a handful of men widely separated from any support, with Foy's division both in front and flank, which rendered our only safety in an instant retreat. But before the Battalion went to the rightabout a round shot from the opposite side of the river took down 10 men of the battalion, 1 dragoon and 2 horses. A Sergeant of our company, of the name of Thornton, who had 3 or 4 days' crop of beard, had seized on the opportunity to reap and had just concluded his favourite lilt of 'Tom Toldrum knows that his uncle is well, etc', with his face in the suds, while the razor was rasping away over the cheek which contained the quid[14], when the round shot mentioned struck the column. Tom jumps up and says, 'There I am,' throwing the shaving implements into the knapsack, bundles it up and off he goes. But the sight of Tom half-shaved and half-suds was truly laughable. Nor did he get the remainder shorn for two days afterwards. Our poor Pipe Major happened to be one of the wounded, having his right arm carried away and the only lament made for him was 'Old split the whistle has done'. So in my opinion, he paid too dear for his whistle.

The river ran here in a curved direction and in the shade of some trees, on the opposite bank, the enemy had planted their guns unobserved, which they used to good effect, the cavalry fording the river at the same time, while a flanking fire of round and grape urged us on in double quick time, in making for the bridge crossing the canal, which was both narrow and bad, but which was the only place passable. The Battalion got more closely locked up than in the open space, which the enemy seemed to be aware of, as they ceased the fire, which I imagined was for the purpose of elevating the guns for the bridge, so that I let the main body pass the bridge before I crossed it. I was not wrong in my conjecture, for as the Battalion was crossing, the guns opened up in great style, but almost every shot flew over the column.

It had been stated in the history of the Peninsular War, but it is not the fact, that the enemy gathered up abundance of baggage and prisoners on the field. As to our baggage, it was left with the Division, while we made the excursion. Consequently it was not within their grasp, and even had they got every ounce that belonged to the Battalion, it would have fallen far short of abundance. And as to prisoners I was nearly the last man over the bridge, and I am quite confident we did not lose a single man as prisoner with the exception of those who fell badly wounded, and whom it was impossible to get away.

*   *   *

After passing the bridge two Spanish grasshoppers[15] came up and opened a well directed fire on the advancing cavalry, which enabled the Battalion to get clear without further loss. I mentioned my being nearly the last man over the bridge, so the cavalry being pretty nigh, Captain Stewart gallops up, and laying hold of my hand, clapping spurs to the mule he whirled me along at no measured pace, and soon conducted me out of their reach. Letting go his herculean grasp, he cries, 'Now up the side of the mountain and you're safe.' I was now joined by an old schoolfellow, William Gorman[16]. 'By the books Douglas,' says he, 'I can go no further.' Being unwilling to let him fall into their hands while a chance remained, I ran down to the canal where there was some water and brought up a refreshment in the shape of a cupful. We swallowed a little, and to the hill we took, and the cavalry were close at our heels.

Again we joined the Division, but since our departure in the morning the face of affairs had considerably changed. The enemy had now occupied the dry canal in great numbers, which General Oswald[17] ought to have done. The bridge over the Carrion was blown (or rather down). Yet to the left of the town it was fordable for cavalry but not infantry. So each horseman took up an infantryman behind him and landed (I cannot say altogether safe) on Terra Firma. In this manner was the dry canal lined with French infantry, under the protection of a cross fire from the opposite side of the town, which here ran mainly in the form of the letter 'A'. To let them remain in this situation would have been next to madness, as they were increasing every minute, and not likely to be agreeable companions during the night.

On Wellington's coming to the hill which commanded a full view of the scene of attack and defence, he ordered our Brigade to drive the enemy from their snug berth down the hill. The Royals[18] and the 38th went, which was none of the easiest jobs as it was very steep and broken. The fire of the enemy slackened on seeing us move down, until we came on a level with their guns, and then the play began. Our first fire and advancing with the bayonet cleared the canal and here, if Wellington's orders had been obeyed, our loss would have been trifling as we were to halt and keep possession of it and then it would have been impossible for those dispossessed of their lodging to have escaped, as they became exposed to the two fires. But, instead of occupying this post, we were ordered to follow the fugitives to the river's brink, exposed to a front and flanking fire of round and grape shot with occasional shells. One of the latter fell close to Lieut McKillegan and he very wisely threw himself on the ground when it exploded, killed 5 and wounded a great many more. The enemy were driven to the river's brink and all were either killed, wounded or made prisoners. Indeed, there were very few of the latter class. We now fell back into the canal under a cloud of bullets. On the bank Col Campbell's horse received a bullet between the shoe and hoof which caused it to kick most unmercifully. Dismounting and looking to see where the animal was hurt, he exclaimed (while his eyes flashed like fire), 'What ails the bugger'.[19]

We took up our lodgings here for the night but were greatly annoyed with shells as long as light remained. At dusk we threw out our pickets, having sentries close to the river to prevent surprise, and dare not so much as light a pipe while the boys on the other side (we could distinctly see by the light of the fires) were making themselves quite at home. The night was very cold, and having no means of keeping ourselves warm, it set sore on the old Ague men from Walcheren. Before night we could hear the guns and baggage on the move, and as day began to dawn our pickets were called in and we resumed our march to the front.

Pursued by the French
The wine vaults ranged along the side of the hills appeared like straggling villages. Their appearance resembled the Norman windows which you may have seen in old-fashioned buildings. The tempting juice which lay concealed in these labyrinths, which were from 80 to 100 steps below the surface, were not proof against the soldiers. It must not be understood that we were marching through a country such as old Ireland, but bad on roads; under our half-shod feet[20] plunging through rivers and morasses, nearly shirtless, while with regard to our coats and trousers, if they deserved the name, I am fully confident that a cart load of them would not be allowed to decorate the walls at the *Paddle*.[21] Add to this a keen appetite, without the means of satisfying it, with an enemy pushing on at the point of the bayonet, and then condemn us for a little wine, which was the only thing that kept the spunk in us. I appeal to any man who shared in the privations of the Peninsular campaigns whether or not I have stated the facts. From hearing the accounts of plunder perpetrated on this retreat, many would naturally conclude that the British Army acted the part of bandit more than the soldier, and that he is little better than an ass held in chains, that when unshackled is as ferocious as a tiger. It's easy for a few individuals, met perhaps to spend an evening in festivity, and who may have been favoured with details of these distressing scenes, glossed over by barely pointing out the length of the march, etc, to censor the army without taking into account the hunger, the hardships, the cold and nakedness, which we endured. Then, and then only, let their verdict be given . . .

After passing Valladolid, the bridges being all destroyed, we had a little repose. Our Quartermaster had made shift to restore our uniforms, but want of conveyance obliged him to halt. In this dilemma he wrote to the Colonel who acquainted his Lordship with this situation, which had become critical, as General Hill[22] was retiring from Madrid in that direction.[23] No time was to be lost. Accordingly we were ordered to march for our refit, which was no unwelcome news, being 2 years in arrears; so that in 19 cases out of 20 it would have required judges of no ordinary capacity to determine the original colour of either coat or trousers. In two days we reached Arevalo, piled arms in the streets, and broke open boxes, barrels and bales. Each man received a suit on the spot. It might happen that a man of 5 feet 3 would get a suit fit for a grenadier, while the more unfortunate grenadier had to thrust himself into something like what mad people are decorated with (a straitjacket). Thus we were clean once more; the old weatherbeaten rags we left for the Spaniards to amuse themselves with.

As General Hill was on the retreat from Madrid, it was expected that the whole British and Portuguese Army would be concentrated between Valladolid and Arevalo. But the bridges being replaced sooner than his Lordship expected and Hill not having joined with us, together with the enemy extending on our right, left no choice but to fall back to keep our communications open with Salamanca and Ciudad Rodrigo. After receiving our refit, we fell in and marched to join the Army again then falling back on our old, but glorious field of Salamanca. Wellington offered them battle on nearly the old soil, but no. Marmont had received a lesson on that ground which the whole of the French Generals would not easily forget, and made them rather delicate in coming to close quarters again. I believe the French soldiers were eager for battle, willing no doubt to wipe off some of the stains which their character had received for coming in contact with the British. But be assured, though destitute in every comfort and worn down with fatigue, they would have found their mistake had we come to blows, as the army were as savage as a bear robbed of her whelps; and though not in the complete order, I think they were in greater humour for fighting, and I feel confident that no army ever retired before the enemy with so much reluctance than did the British from Salamanca to Ciudad Rodrigo.

We marched from Arevalo at 9 at night with fixed bayonets, not being very confident whether we were marching into the enemy's lines. However, we kept on until we came in view of the encampment. This may seem curious, to see an encampment at night; the mystery, however, is easily solved, as it was seen and known by the number of fires; but to our no small satisfaction, it proved to be General Hill's army. Thus, after marching 5 leagues in 5 hours and 10 minutes, without a halt, during which not a man fell out, we joined the army again, being now out of the grasp of the enemy.

We had a little repose. The weather had now become very wet, and the country between Salamanca and Ciudad Rodrigo, being generally flat, we had most miserable spots to encamp on. If inclined to sleep we were obliged to repose like so many turkeys, on the branches of trees, to keep us out of the water and mud. On our first march from Salamanca we received a draft of 250 men. Poor wretches! I pitied them. Being unaccustomed to such work, they stood in mid-leg shivering with cold, not knowing what to do.

The pig shooting went on very briskly; so much so that we were at times ready to form square against cavalry, thinking the enemy were at hand. The French cavalry were considerably in advance of our flanks, so we were obliged to march in column of companies through these wilds and morasses, which to any one except soldiers would have been impassable. Every movable article, being in front, had so cut up the roads . . . or any opening through the woods, that we were not only mid-leg, but knee-deep in mud, yet the men plodded this cheerless way with cheerfulness. It occurred to my mind that the region resembled the land where Cain went to reside after the curse was invoked[24], for certainly very few footprints were visible and some places, I am certain, never bore such an impress. On the 2nd day's march from Salamanca, a woman a little to the right of the column had sunk under the hardships and expired, but her infant was still alive; and a little further on the left a Portuguese soldier, worn with hunger and fatigue, had also sunk in the mud and was totally unable to extricate himself. Though not more than 50 yards off no assistance could be given as the means of conveyance[25] on our front was as far off as Ciudad Rodrigo. Our adjutant made an attempt to rescue him by riding up and taking hold of his hand, but to no purpose. There he was left, and most likely it was his grave as the enemy were close at hand who, be well assured, would not give themselves more trouble with him than we, but expend a ball upon him rather than a biscuit.

On the last day's march we plunged through the River Huebra; just in time as the enemy's guns opened on us in great style while in the water, while a host of skirmishers extended along the rugged banks, keeping up a very sharp fire. The French followed no further, and we reached the hills near Ciudad in peace, on the 19th November.

On the road to Celirico

It was most fortunate for me that the retreat had terminated, as on the last day's march the sinews of my right foot protruded through the skin, which would have been the means of my being made an inmate of a French prison, had the retreat continued another day.

The fine gardens around Ciudad Rodrigo were plundered of their last head of cabbage by those in charge of the baggage, etc being sent on in front, batmen[26] and stragglers of the army and which fell to the lot of the whole army to pay for. Now it is these and such like that brings disgrace on an army. Though the word 'army' includes every individual, no man of common sense could, or would, leave his ranks to look for plunder, or if he did it would be running the risk of his neck. In many cases the innocent suffer with the guilty, as the main body of the army never had a mouthful, nor were they within 30 miles or upwards of where it was cooked, yet all had to bear their part in the disgrace and payment.

From Ciudad Rodrigo we marched to a place called Campillo, which proved to be one of the hungriest headquarters of misery that ever fell to the lot of the British soldier to encamp on. For 3 days and as many nights, not a toothful in the shape of eatables was served out. Providentially round the camp there were vast quantities of sloes and acorns, as served to keep the spunk alive; though this astringent food had like to have cost a good number of men their lives. The few days halt here showed very plainly what would be the result of all our fatigues, as the men sickened very fast. At length we marched for winter cantonments, Lanrego being headquarters for the Division, while the different regiments were dispersed among the villages around. The morning we marched from Campillo, I was sent in charge of three wagon loads of sick to Celirico. On the first day's march one of my charge died at Villa Formosa, where we left him for the Guards[27] to bury. Our guide, not being too well acquainted with the track across the plains of Almeida, we lost our way and the first place

63

we found ourselves entering was the town of Trendada, Head-quarters for the Army, this being out of our line of march, yet no way displeasing, as it afforded the prospect of getting some place of shelter. But our prospects vanished on entering the town, as we could not get as much shelter as would cover a donkey. Thus we were obliged to retire and spread our blankets under some olive trees for the night, lit our fires and made ourselves as comfortable as circumstances would admit.

I took good care to make out a ration return during the night, and urged by a good appetite started at daylight to draw them from the Commissary, whose store we were directed to by the bells on the mules, having as many of the waggon train with me as could be spared from the sick for the purpose of carrying them.[28] While awaiting the arrival of the storekeeper a host of muleteers and mules surrounded a little chapel which had been converted into a store; one of the muleteers was eating a piece of bread, and in full conversation with some others, when the poor mule reached out his head and broke bread with him, this kind of comradeship not being quite agreeable to the muleteer, who gave it a clumsy thump on the nose. In a few minutes he made free with a second mouthful, when in a rage the muleteer seized the animal by the trappings on the head and with a stone – I dare say 4 lbs in weight – he belaboured it on the nose and mouth till I really thought he would not leave a tooth in its head. On letting him loose he cries, 'Cares maise'; (that is, 'Do you want any more?'). Up comes another to water his beast at a fountain close at hand, but the animal refused. Here the stubborn temper of the mule was quite overcome by the barbarity of the man, as he beat him as the other had done, and when wearied with these gentle reproofs, he laid hold of his nose with his teeth, dragging his head to the water until he actually made him drink. I have often heard say that one man may take a horse to the water, but 20 cannot make him drink, but in this case it was a mule, and the man scarcely deserved the name.

We received our rations and once more had enough and to spare, as the poor sick fellows would make use of little or none. However, we packed it up in the wagons, and to the road we went. We had scarcely proceeded a league when we were nearly prevented from proceeding by a stream of water, both deep and broad, which ran across the road. In short, it was completely inundated. Here our front wagons got through in safety, but the second did not fare so well, as one half remained in the stream and the other at the horses' tails, while the poor sick fellows were, with no little difficulty, fished out in a miserable plight and placed against a stone fence to dry; while with the other two waggons we made for a village, got housed, and returned for our half-drowned companions. Having all got into shelter, 2 more of my charge died through the course of the night. Having remained here two days, we proceeded to Celirico; with our crazy overloaded waggons we made our way but slowly. It was now after sunset and a league and a half to march ere we were to get lodgings. One of the sick wished to walk a little and was indulged, I having to keep him company, but we got to the rear and lost sight of the main body. An old shepherd driving his flock to the fold, my sick man seized a fine lamp and clap't it under his greatcoat.

We turned to our right, which led to a village, but no soldiers were there. 'Twas now dark and we were puzzled as to what to do. We were directed to a river at the end of the village where we might cross. It certainly might have been passable in daylight, but in the dark it required a steady head. The bridge consisted of large planks, or rather one plank about a foot broad. After looking in vain for a proper bridge, we found that cross we must, or remain there all night. We made the attempt. I slung Brown Bess on my shoulder and for greater security sat down on the planks, moving or creeping as well as I could until I gained the opposite side, after which my companion crossed in a similar way, that is rode the plank. But the worst of it was, he being weak in rising up, staggered a little and I endeavoured to prevent his falling in. My shoulder strap gave way and in went my firelock, in endeavouring to recover which we were both near being drowned, but ultimately we recovered her. Here we were in a nice mess. To the road we went, but after wandering about for some time we gave over the idea of finding our companions that night. So down with the knapsack, out with the blanket and we lay down in the shelter of a stone fence to have a nap. But being so wet, and the night so cold, with the rain which beat in on our faces, prevented anything in the shape of repose. Up we started again, and had not proceeded half a mile when fortune threw a pizzano in our way. I made inquiry concerning the sick and had the consolation of hearing they were entering the next village. Being ignorant of the road, I asked the old chap to act as guide, which he steadily refused. Fixing the bayonet I gave him his choice, either to show the road or get skewered. So, scratching his head, he led the way, and strange to say the waggons entered one end of the village while

65

we entered the other. All now being right we got stowed away and made an excellent mess of our lamb.

In Hospital

We arrived without further incident at Celirico where, after giving up my charge, the Doctor wished me to remain and take charge of the sick and wounded of the Division. But I retained in memory the epithets that are thrown out on those who were too eager to fill such situations, and in general in no great hurry to rejoin their Regiment and who could in general spin a yarn far superior to those who were already present with their Regiment and no way affected with that terrible disorder well known in the army by name of cannon fodder. Contrary to his wishes I positively refused his offer, when the doctor (Prosser) told me he would not draw rations for me on the march if I insisted on joining the Regiment, and as my foot was in a bad state, I would be compelled to remain, as a last shift. I told him I would beg my way to the Regiment rather than remain behind. This discourse being overheard by an old Captain of our Company (Beard), who had exchanged into the 11th Foot and happened to be in the same quarters, called me in and handed me 5 dollars, to assist me on the road. It would not be easy to form an idea of what I felt on the occasion, a soldier excepted. Penniless, without a biscuit in my old haversack, in a country partly desecrated, the few remaining inhabitants like weathercocks, always welcoming the prevailing party with '*vivas*', and now after our retreat not too well disposed towards us, or even to let us have what we stood in need of even for money. Yet in the depth of winter I plodded my way and joined the regiment at a village called Burtegande.

I had scarcely joined, when I was warned for guard. I made known to the Sergeant Major the bad state of my foot, wishing to have a day's rest, but received the conciliatory answer, 'You must do your duty or go to the hospital.' Thus, you see there was a choice, and to hospital I went, in which, being so crowded, I was obliged to sleep with a man in a high fever, and I may truly say I was completely inoculated with the disorder. My second day of repose was spent on our bed of indian corn straw, which indeed was a luxury, yet at the same time it was scarcely one remove from lying on sticks. This, with our weatherbeaten blanket, with scarcely as much wool as would conceal the carcass of a flea, formed our bed. I wish my readers to understand that then, and even now, I do not complain, and if I had complained what would

66

have been the use? I had the same as my comrades, and I could expect no more. But I merely mention it that it may be seen what soldiers endure, or have endured on the Peninsula. The fever which I had caught was of a most malignant nature, so much so as left the Surgeon no hopes of my recovery; and as it is generally the case when men are at the point of death, they are ordered to get anything they desire. And thus it was with me, as the Surgeon left orders with the Hospital Sergeant to let me have whatever I wanted. Fortunately, the captain of my company called and left 2 guineas for me with the Hospital Sergeant, who enquired what I would like to have. 'Half a gallon of mulled wine,' was the reply. This medicine was sent for, mulled and in the space of one hour I drained the last and something more to the bargain. This, you may depend upon, was none of the least of doses, and on the Doctor's visit he pronounced me out of danger. To the poor fellow who attended me and behaved like a brother, I made . . . a present of 3 dollars, and he being in a convalescent state, got liberty from the surgeon for 2 days leave; at the expiry of which he returned rather unwell, lay down in my bed, and in 2 days was no more. His name, which shall ever be dear to me, was Jeremiah Dempsey. He appeared to have had a tolerable share of education. In using the pen, which he could wield to perfection, and in his native tongue (the Irish) addressed all his letters to his friends.

I Rejoin the Battalion

'Twas now our fatigues began to exhibit themselves in all the forms of sickness, while numbers lost their toes, some their limbs, and not a few their lives, their long neglected sores having turned to mortification.[29] I now began to recover my strength, though slowly, and was able in March to do duty once more. From this village [Burtegande] we marched to another named Marzon Trea. I omitted to mention the death of our own Chaplain, who through his great anxiety in administering spiritual comfort to the dying soldiers, caught the fever and died lamented by all, even the most profligate, and his dying request was to be interred on the spot where he used to preach to the soldiers, a request which was punctually attended to.

The period of service of a number of men who had taken on for 7 years was now drawing to a close, and to part from them now would have drained our ranks of a number of seasoned soldiers. An order arrived for those of the 7 years' service to extend their service. It was really laughable to see the Drum Major with his cap decorated with ribbons, going through all the ceremonies of recruiting as in a county fair, endeavouring to prevail on them to renew their bond for 7 years or life. The greater part, after all their hardships, signed on again, receiving one half of the bounty, which caused fine sprees, the wine being good and cheap on the banks of the Douro; so much so that the drunken fellows boiled the beef in it, which rendered it unfit for anyone. It was customary for the Portuguese to subtract a small measure out of each pint. Though small – not more than 3 thimbles full – still it was not very agreeable to the British. This toll, it appeared, went towards the support of the monks, and when interrogated as to what purpose it was applied, the answer was 'For Saint Antonio'. I shocked the feelings of my landlady one day most unmercifully, by telling her that Saint Antonio was a great drunkard if he made use of all the wine they took in his name. This was carrying the joke too far. Nor could she forgive me during our sojourn in the village.

The Portuguese, generally speaking, like a good many, wore two faces. It would appear they loved the British troops, and a just right they had in so doing, as through them their country was delivered from tyranny and oppression. And yet they considered it no sin to take away the life which had been hazarded for their protection if that life displeased. They considered it no greater crime to kill a British subject than one of their dogs. They generally carried a large knife concealed up the sleeve of the coat, and be assured they knew how to handle it. But it was a matter of no small amusement to see them engage to box, as this kind of pastime was to them rather novel; so in facing their man they struck with their open hand, while every blow from our own lads told so unmercifully that in a few minutes the battle ended with the poor Portuguese's features being no way improved.

It is not easy for anyone unaccustomed to the Army to conceive of the tricks which some soldiers will put into practice, and with such seeming honesty, that were the following not well authenticated, it would be set down as a fictitious story. In the winter of 1812 we were paid in English gold and of course the value made known to the Portuguese authorities, so that no advantage might be taken on either side. After the sickness had subsided, we lived in what I may call style, and ready for another campaign. The town of Lamego is certainly fine, considering that it is a Portuguese town, with a good market. One day a man of our Light Company, named Roger McGowan, took post convenient to a woman who was busily engaged vending her goods, and in the midst of her hurry had taken a guinea, which happened to be crooked. This did not escape the eye of the Light Company man, who had taken up some article, and in a little time, when he got her busy, demanded the truck, or change. The poor woman inquired what truck, seeming enraged at the question. He broke into the most violent passion calling her in half English and half Portuguese anything but a lady. The boisterous behaviour of the soldier attracted a mob. When the Adjutant Cluff and Lieut Balfour, passing that way and seeing this well known character in this turmoil, wished to know what was wrong, half-stifled with rage he informed them of having purchased the article he held, and given her a guinea, she refusing to let him have the change. They were pretty well aware, judging, no doubt from his former good conduct[30], he had not given the money, as well as the woman's version of the story. Thinking to puzzle him, the Adjutant says, 'Had you any mark on your guinea that you would know it again?' Immediately he cries out, 'Yes, I would know it above all guineas in the world, its crooked.' On this the woman was ordered to empty her purse, and out tumbles the crooked guinea. Shouting out at the sight, 'There it is', the poor woman stood thunderstruck, while her crooked guinea was carried away in triumph by the very man that was as near as possible giving me dry lodgings in a French prison the first night of our retreat from Burgos.

Chapter Five

The Battle of Vitoria and Siege of San Sebastian

Wellington had spent the winter of 1812–13 in the area of Ciudad Rodrigo rebuilding his army with welcome reinforcements from England and planning his next offensive.

In May, 1813, as Douglas relates, the army was once more on the march, advancing three columns up. The left and largest column, under Graham, consisted of six British divisions, two Portuguese brigades and a strong force of cavalry. In the centre, under Wellington's personal command, were two British divisions and one Spanish with supporting cavalry. Hill was on the right with two British divisions. Graham turned the French flank on the Couro, forcing the enemy, who were under Joseph Bonaparte's personal command, to withdraw to the Ebro, Burgos falling to the Allies without a fight. Graham's task had been greatly helped by the fact that although the French still had numerical superiority, the quality of their forces had deteriorated because Napoleon had withdrawn many of their best and most experienced troops into France to compensate for his appalling losses in Russia in 1812. Furthermore, the period of refurbishment and reinforcement which the British had enjoyed in the winter had given Wellington's army a considerable boost.

On 14 and 15 June Wellington crossed the Ebro on the French right and by the 20th, having concentrated his army, was facing Joseph at Vitoria, where he attacked on the 21st, utterly routing the French, capturing most of their guns and all their baggage train. For this great victory he was promoted Field Marshal and created Duke of Vitoria by the Spanish.

Despite a deplorable failure in eastern Spain by General

Murray, who had raised the siege of Tarragona for some inexplicable reason, Wellington now closed up to the French frontier. Meanwhile, Napoleon had removed his brother from command and replaced him by Soult, who now advanced in strength on 24 July to relieve the fortresses of San Sebastian and Pamplona, the former of which was already under the first stages of siege. Near Sorauren, Soult was defeated by the British in battle but pressed on towards San Sebastian, leaving Marshal Reille to face Wellington, who promptly attacked him and administered another defeat, in consequence of which Soult withdrew into France, hotly pursued by Hill. Thus the two passes over the Pyrenees were restored to Wellington, who now turned his personal attention to San Sebastian, which he stormed on 31 August. Douglas was severely wounded in the leg during the siege and evacuated to England. After very hard fighting, the garrison capitulated on 8 September.

*   *   *

We commenced our march in May, facing the enemy once more. The left wing of the army was commanded by the hero of Barossa[1], and as all our advances were marked with hunger, so this was nearly as bad as the advance to Almeida in 1811. As we approached Vitoria, our rations grew scarcer, until not a mouthful was to be had for man or beast. One night, having halted on a fine plain of a gravelly nature and for rations got turned into a field of beans in 20 minutes time the ground was as bare as the hour it was ploughed. To rest we went, but in the course of the night it commenced to rain and blow most tremendously, and as I before observed, the ground being of a gravelly nature, the tent pegs were uprooted and down came our house on top of us. Each man was eager to have a sleep, and each and all wished to have the tent pitched again. Yet no one would stir, so there we lay; the water soaking through left both men and accoutrements in a miserable plight on the bugles calling us to renew our labour at daylight. The sight of the men encamping from under the tents exceeded anything, almost anything, that could be conceived in the shape of misery. Benumbed with cold, drenched to the skin, hungry as wolves, without the means of any kind of comfort, or the most distant hopes of relief unless providence would interfere and send us a little provisions, at the conclusion of the day's march we had the good fortune to have about half a pound of wheat per man, which was a welcome guest.

The day following, being the 18th June, we fell in with the enemy, who were on the march for Bilbao. We met near the crossroads leading to that town from the village of Orma. Here our old animosity kindled into a flame, and to work we went. The French appeared to be in good heart and played their part well, but getting flanked by our taking the village of Orma, they cut off the engagement and made direct for Vitoria after a very light skirmish. Two unfortunate corporals, who had extended their service in winter quarters, lost both their limbs by a round shot, but died during the operation of amputation. When the poor fellows fell, some of the boys sang out, 'The other half of the bounty is paid'.[2] We pursued our march, halted on the 20th to allow the Commissary to come up if possible, but no, and as a last shift we were obliged to send out parties through the country to try to collect a little grub. This day was spent in gloomy forebodings and many a long look out for rations, but in vain. The morning of the 21st arrived and with it the party which had been sent to collect bread and they brought a timely supply which accounted to nearly a pound per man.

Vitoria

This was in the nick of time, for before it was divided the word was given, 'Stand to your arms'. Hill had commenced the spree. On the right the grasshoppers were hammering away. We divided our mess on the march. My comrade and I very soon demolished one share, resolving to keep the other until we encamped at night. As we arrived on the main road leading to Vitoria, a stream of water crossed it. The big guns were now in full play. I says to the comrade (Baum), 'Let us finish the other share, for whoever lives tonight will have plenty.'[3] On this the bread underwent a plunge bath in the stream, which caused it to go down a little quicker and easier and thus concluded our repast, in strong hopes of a second course in a short time.

In a little time we arrived at the top of a hill, and here the town of Vitoria appeared in full view, surrounded by columns of French cavalry and infantry. We halted a few minutes, viewing the field which was destined to add another leaf to the wreath of England's triumphs. General Hill, on our right, would be master of the heights, while the French very ably disputed his title. We were not kept long idle. We marched to the village of Gamara. We drew up in column within gunshot of the village, primed and loaded, uncased the colours, and on we went to the attack. As we stood

72

in column, a Brigade of Portuguese, on our right, had attracted the attention of the boys in the village, who let fly a few 9 pounders among them, one of which struck the trunk of a tree and caused it to roll to the right of our Regiment so smoothly that one of our grenadiers put out his foot to stop it, which shattered his leg in such a manner that amputation became necessary, and he died in the operation. His name was Patrick Cain. We moved to the village under no small fire. The road, being fine, enabled us to move in column of companies on our right. The country towards Vitoria was open, but somewhat defended by the zig-zag course of the River Zadora. On our left there was a large thorn hedge in full feather, through which the balls were whizzing very thick, as you might perceive the leaves and branches falling fast, and here and there a man.

We reached the village, which we named Gomorrah, as it was a scene of fire and brimstone. The enemy were driven through the village, and over the River Zadora. One wing cleared the houses and gardens on the right and then lined the bank of the river, keeping up a heavy fire on the advancing supports. The light company entered a house at the end of the bridge, from the windows of which a very destructive fire was then kept up, while as many as could pushed across and formed as they arrived close to an old chapel. We that had crossed had taken up a very favourable position and were picking them off in good style. Here there appeared to be some want. Had the regiments which entered the village been pushed across the bridge at the time we crossed and established a firm footing on the opposite bank, the right wing of the French army would have been separated from the left, and, thus situated, the wreck of the French would have been nearly as bad as Waterloo. The enemy seemed to know the value of this spot and poured down a heavy fire on the few that got over and so obliged us to retrace our steps. The day was uncommonly warm and many ran down to the river for drink, numbers of which fell in the water, and not a few badly wounded were carried away by the stream. In advancing across the bridge, best man foremost, exposed to a heavy fire which raked it, and from a flanking fire from the right, one of the 4th Regiment and I were close together when he received a ball in the head, and down he went. Contrary to my expectations I cleared it and on turning the corner of the house occupied by our light company a ball struck a stone close to my head and rebounding lodged on my skull. Well, I really thought all the world was in a blaze around me, and there

I stood, for some time unconscious of everything, but when I got the use of my eyes I found I was on my feet and not much the worse.

The enemy made several attempts to retake the village, but were met with such a shower of shot that they abandoned the idea. Two of our 9 pounders stationed at a stone cross swept the bridge. Being separated from my company I had to cross the street, so trailing arms I marched across unhurt, though you would imagine a sparrow could not escape. After joining we were preparing for a grand push at the bridge (but too late), which had to be cleared of the dead by throwing them into the river, to make way for the guns. The French had abandoned two guns at the end of the bridge. In the tumbrel[4] of one a lad of ours found 160 Doubloons.[5]

As we were forming in the gardens, a hen which seemed to have lost his way was pursued by several of the men, and ran for shelter to a thorn hedge in rear of which was a stone wall; just as two of them were making the grasp at her, a French 9 pounder interfered and carried her off a legal prize. By the time they had given way on the right and the cavalry had begun to act on the open ground the pursuit became general. There is one thing certain. The French won the race, though the commanding officers of the different regiments urged on the men by calling out at the top of the voice, 'Forward . . . (such a regiment),' till the whole army was rushing on as fast as their ass-like loads would admit of. Together with the heat of the day this soon exhausted us of nearly the last puff of wind.

After so warm and well contested a race, it may be easily imagined that a halt became indispensable to renew the wind in our exhausted bellows. Accordingly, by the skirt of a wood we made a halt and threw out our pickets, and then started to look for something in the shape of eatables. A small village was close at hand, but the principal houses were occupied by the General Officers and their staff. Yet even this protection was not proof against hunger. One house in particular was occupied by General Hay (who had just lost his son, a fine young man, Captain of our light company and aide-de-camp to his father; he was killed by grape shot in crossing the bridge at Gamara Major. Into this house the prowling wolves entered, and finding some wheat and flour, a light became necessary. But the struggle was so severe as to who would get most that the light was unheeded and, making contact with some rubbish, the house was in flames in a few minutes. The old general, running out, exclaims, 'What would I think of it but my own Regiment to set fire to the house over my head.' However, house or no house, the point in question was the belly.

The plunder to be obtained was immense. You would actually imagine that all the carriages in Spain were collected round Vitoria. The plain was covered with books, papers, cannon ammunition, wagons, tumbrels, etc., while doubloons and dollars were as plentiful as gooseberries in a fair.[6] Many of the stragglers got overloaded with these shining articles, and falling on them in the rear the Spaniards made no scruple to ease them of their money and, in case of resistance, the life too.

The first mess that I and my comrade got ready was a kettle full of flour and water, or more plainly speaking paster[7] which went down with a good relish even without salt. The second course was more palatable, such as young pigs, fowl, etc, which, being in such abundance, I sat up all night cooking.

San Sebastian: I am Wounded

Our Adjutant was no great admirer of those who made it a point to keep clear of scrapes, or in other words skulked in hospitals. Just in front of our Regiment the Commissary had halted with his stores, having a Corporal of ours attached to him as conductor.[8] Of course he was out of the Adjutant's grasp, being on duty. But seeing a noted character rather convenient to run tasks, steps up and accosting the Corporal says, 'Well, Corporal Teal, what are you doing?' 'Nothing,' was the reply. 'And you, Mr so-and-so, what are you doing?' 'Helping Corporal Teal, sir.' 'Oh very well, so Corporal Teal is doing nothing and you are helping him. Pray be so kind as to rejoin your company.'[9]

We marched the next day, the 22nd, and the only man remaining of a draft of 250 men which joined us on the retreat from Burgos, between Salamanca and Ciudad Rodrigo, fell out of the ranks. We followed the enemy by way of Silvetera, and as is commonly the case after an action, the rain descended in torrents, while we had to pass on through the town to find the softest side of the stone for a pillow. We were now on the road for Pamplona, but received orders to retrace our steps and lay siege to San Sebastian. We fell back on Vitoria and Tolosa. We encamped close outside, being on the strength of the Provost Guard in the suburbs. A lot of gamblers, chiefly of Portuguese, were hammering away at the cards close by, for be it remembered the Portuguese are pretty expert at them. A few Spanish pizzanos were tempted to engage. (These gamblers were just such a description of fellows as our thimble men[10].) The doubloons were thrown down in lots. Mr Red Hackle[11], hearing such a noise, looks out, and seeing what was going on ordered me to take all the money from them and send them about their business, an order which was promptly obeyed. And very well contented they were to escape.

The road leading to San Sebastian, considering the wild mountainous tracks, was in places beautiful, particularly around the villages. Arnany is one of the most considerable, neatly built, with a good market, and lying about 3 leagues from the garrison. At this time – the beginning of July – the plums, cherries, etc were in full feather, while the country around San Sebastian was one continued wood of apple trees. We pitched our camp on the slope of a hill within gunshot of the town, but hid from the view of San Sebastian as we were now on the sea coast. We had abundance of rations. The sight of the sea was so novel that the men could with difficulty be restrained from ascending the hill to look at it, and would sit enjoying the sight as if looking at their native shore. Here the vegetables were pretty plentiful and good, and though not regularly served out we were not always short of a little mutton, so that I may say we lived like what we were – fighting cocks.

*   *   *

A large convent which the enemy had fortified was the first object of attack, against which 6 eighteen pounders were directed. We broke ground against the convent on the 12th July, erected a battery for the 6 guns in question, and soon began to play. The French seemed very determined here, for as the wall began to give way to the fire, the French soldiers were seen frequently, after the ball had passed through the wall, to fire through the place, thus using it as a loophole. This was the only place I ever knew the French to behave dishonourably in respect of firing on sentries, numbers of whom they killed.

The convent was breached and taken, with considerable loss. A large burial ground lay to the right of the convent, just to the rear of the village of St Martin. The ground lay high and extended from the convent to the extremity of the village, which was built close to or underneath it. A wall on the brow of the hill above the village served to conceal from the enemy the work carried on in the burial ground, which was laid out for a battery of 15 twenty-fours, 6 mortars and 2 howitzers. During these preparations the enemy were not idle in letting us have plenty of shot and shell. The trenches commenced at the gate of the convent and ran in a zig-zag fashion towards a fieldwork, called the half-moon battery, of field pieces. These, though small, annoyed us most unmercifully, as all our approaches had to be thieflike in the dark. At the least spark of fire from a pick, axe or spade it would be your wisdom to lie down as close to the ground and as quickly as possible, and endeavour to escape the shower of grape levelled at the spot. Not that this precaution had the desired effect at all times, as a great many were killed and wounded.

On the opposite side of the river, on the passage side, a battery of 10 twenty-fours were in as forward a state as ours. A wall ran from the extreme right of St Martin, over which the water which supplied the French garrison was conveyed. To cut off the water we ran a trench completely through the ruins of this destroyed village, to reach the wall from the last house. It did not exceed 20 yards, but we were completely deluged with shot from the half-moon battery. Lieut Armstrong commanded the working party, who did their utmost to dig a hole for shelter from this incessant fire but to no purpose as the earth was battered down as soon as raised, and scarcely a man left unhurt. Whilst the last man was creeping through the doorway from the trench, a shot carried his foot away, while the poor fellow sung out most lustily, 'Worrah, worrah, worrah'.

Thus the idea of cutting off their supply of water for the present had to be given up until such time as the half-moon battery was taken. Those who escaped unhurt were assembled in the shelter of the walls, yet here was no safety as the shot flew through the windows and doors, and, rebounding off the walls, hurt many, while stones and mortar falling in every direction bruised some and blinded others. The entrenching tools and firelocks of those who were wounded being left in the trench, Lieut Armstrong[12], wishing to save them, asked for volunteers, while he headed them. I instantly offered my service. We both leapt into the trench and succeeded in securing 14 items, under such a shower of round shot as actually covered us with clouds of sand. Yet we came off unhurt. We had scarcely got in shelter when a large shell dropped on the floor, rolling about, the fuse blazing. Armstrong stood looking at it, when I laid hold of him and dragged him to the rear of a broken wall, at nearly the instant it exploded. Thus his life was saved for that time.

Our batteries were now in a forward state. The wall in front of the graveyard in a great measure concealed the working parties. Still, I suppose the enemy suspected something to be going on there, as they generally sent us a regular share of shot and shell, which obliged us to have a sentry on the lookout whose business was to give the men at work notice of shot or shell, in order to take shelter in rear of the splinter proofs (large piles of earth left in rear of the platforms, proof against shot or shell) and to call out 'shot' or 'shell', as the case might be. One day a man of our company named Lucas was on the lookout, but unfortunately poor Bobby had an impediment, or stammering in his speech. Seeing a shell from the Castle, he began, 'Shish, shish, shish, shell,' at last, but too late, as it exploded, killed 3 of the 38th and wounded a number more. So Bob had to be relieved. The troops in the trenches were relieved every night at sunset, which was the signal for a general set-to of the garrison. The castle[13], standing so high, had a full view of everything (at least of every movement of the troops) and commanded the town and everything within its reach. 'Tis wonderful how hardened men grow when they are for a length of time exposed, or rather immured, to such dangers. However callous they might be to others, you may be assured that the first law of nature was straitly attended to as far as circumstances would admit of[14]. While moving to our post in the trenches we did so not in slow time, particularly at a point where we became exposed to the fire of the place. A working party one night going down to the trenches, a grenadier of the 59th Regiment had the misfortune to have his head carried away by a shot from the Castle. So instantaneous was death that the trunk stood erect for a few seconds ere it fell. It's no great wonder, a man's head would not be proof against such articles when a good sized tree would be cut down with as much ease as rushes. A great many casualties happened owing to the incessant fire of the garrison, and having through the course of the day pointed guns at the spot where they expected we would break ground[15], every 10 minutes or less throughout the night a shower of grape came whistling along.

The water being cut off from the town, that commodity became very scarce, and as the men in the trenches had to remain 24 hours ere we were relieved, we always carried a quantity of our apples in our haversack to quench our thirst, as no water could be had nigher than the Convent, and to go there it was 20 to one if you would not forget the way back. We used to amuse ourselves by putting an apple on a switch and throwing it into the town. At other times we put our cap on the bayonet and raised it a little above the trench, and in an instant a ball would be through it. When a man was killed in the trench we were obliged to scrape a hole in the sand and tumble him in, as we dare not move out of where we lay. Thus, with the stench of the dead, and the heat of the weather, the trenches actually got lousy. One night, as we were relieving, there were about 10 or 15 yards of the trench exposed to the French battery, which from its black appearance we designated the black battery. If we got over this angle in safety we concluded all's right. The fire of this battery was more destructive than all the rest, and so accurate was their practice that they could take down a single man at any distance within its range. A Corporal of the 38th and I had made a full stop to look at the battery before we made the run, for be assured that one pair of heels at the point was of more value than two pairs of hands, as will be shown. An officer of the 9th Regiment, a little to the rear, comes to the angle of the trench and for bravo would walk on, despising the danger, when a 24 from the battery carried away nearly the whole of his back parts. There he lay, roaring, while the Corporal and I made the run, when another shot buried us in sand, without further injury.

The Spaniards could never forgive us for converting their graveyard into a battery. Most of their dead were tossed about in every direction. There was a curious occurrence which took place one day after the battery opened. A shell from the castle fell into a grave and exploded, tossing the bones of he, or she, in the air, but the skull being driven higher than the other bones, and so perpendicular, that it fell back into the grave from whence it was quickly disinterred.

On the 25th July the breaches were pronounced practicable,[16] but waiting for the tide to be sufficiently low to admit the men to reach the breach, it was daylight ere we moved out of the trenches; and having to keep close to the wall to be clear of the sea as possible; beams of timber, shells, hand grenades and every missile that could annoy or destroy life were hurled from the ramparts on the heads of the men; to shun which, if they kept further out in the tide, showers of grape and musketry swept them away by half-companies. Those who scrambled onto the beach found it was wide and sufficient enough at bottom, but at the top there was not sufficient room for one file at the curtain[17] and from thence to the street was at least 20 feet. This was a house which was on fire close to the breach, and through which our poor fellows were forcing their way, when a shell from our 10-gun battery at the passage side struck the gable and buried nearly a company in the burning ruins. One man alone escaped. The sides of the door being stone fell towards each other, and formed the letter A over him. Though his life was saved by this providential circumstance, he was, I might say, half-roasted, but survived. (I saw him in June 1817, after returning from France, near the potteries in Staffordshire, on the banks of the canal. His face then resembled a new-born infant.[18] His name was John Potts.)

Some little idea may be formed of the destructive fire of the enemy when on the beach were left by the tide more than would have loaded a waggon of fish, killed in the water by the shot of the garrison, as the tide washed the walls of the town. And it not being sufficiently low at the time of the attack those who fell wounded and might have recovered were swept away by the current, which runs here very rapid. Nor was it an easy matter for any man to keep on his feet, as the stones were so slippery. Thus this attempt failed and for some time afterwards it was thought the siege would be abandoned altogether, but the army being successful in front, it was ordered to be renewed, which order was with the greatest alacrity obeyed by every individual concerned, each and all vowing revenge.

Fresh guns arrived from England, and stores of everything requisite. And to work the men went in earnest. Fresh batteries were mounted, one of four 68 lb cannonades, on a hill to the right of the ten-gun battery, where a signal post stood, which could be distinctly seen from France, the shipping keeping a look-out in the rear to prevent supplies from thence, as it was just round the hill. But with all their strictness, the French ships were too many for us; the boats passing to and from the garrison were hailed by the British cruisers[19] and answered in Spanish. Thus, without further investigation, they were suffered to proceed, carrying away the wounded and bringing back whatever they stood in want of.

There was a small conical island close to the mole,[20] in possession of the enemy, and this was the principal quay to the garrison. It was found advisable to take it, which was done by a night attack, though the men on it suffered severely, the heath with which it was clothed taking fire from the bursting of shells which drove them to the water side, to shun the flames as well as the shot of the enemy. 'Twas now they were completely shut up.

August 15th being the anniversary of the birth of Napoleon, at sunset every gun in and around the fortress was fired, which caused considerable alarm in the camp until the cause was known. They fixed in front of the castle, underneath the flagstaff, in very large letters, with lights burning in rear, so that it could be very distinctly read from the trenches (while numbers of the troops were dancing) a banner reading 'Viva Napoleon le Grand.'

Our batteries now opened a 2nd time, and in earnest. In a few days a breach estimated upwards of 60 yards had been made along the face of the place. Fire answering fire of a number of guns was awfully grand, particularly at sunset, before they gave over for the night. From 30 to 40 twenty-fours in a volley went slap into the crumbling walls, while the guns on the town wall were rendered useless, as the men in the trenches kept up an incessant fire by sections and sub-divisions into the gun ports and cut off the gunners if they attempted to work the guns. On Saturday the 30th August 1813, being relieved from the trenches . . . I had the curiosity to go down to the sea side on a gentle declivity, a number of large trees growing on it, about 50 idlers of us looking at the effects of our batteries. And certainly to a reflecting mind the scene was calamitous. There stood the black frowning castle vomiting its thunder in answer to our well supplied batteries, which were tumbling in cart loads, while one of the handsomest towns in Spain (in appearance) sat waiting for the awful sentence to be passed, that was to lay it in ruins ere the next day's sun was set. While viewing this scene of approaching desolation, I observed the enemy bringing a field piece to the waterside, on which I warned the men to get in shelter (as we were all sitting at our ease). Scarcely had we taken the precaution than we were saluted with a few 9 pounders, but without effect. It was very evident from the appearance of the breach that the place must be stormed next day.

We retired in expectation of the order for that event. The last battery erected against a breach was for 4 twenty-fours, on a small mound a little to the right of the front angle to the wall, and within about 20 yards of it. With the greatest labour and fatigue 3 were brought into play, but the 4th remained in the trench completely bogged in the mouldering ruins of those who fell there, and remained so until the town was taken. In the course of the evening the orders were issued and the different Regiments told off for the storm, which was to take place 10 o'clock the following day, Sunday the 31st August. Volunteers for the forlorn hope[21] were called for, and I believe every man nearly wished to go. So many offered their service that in order to satisfy them lots had to be cast. Independent of the Division, a great number of volunteers from other divisions of the army arrived to assist. A number of non-commissioned officers of the brigade met at sunset under some apple trees, for the purpose of bidding goodbye. The liquor went round in full bumpers, to the health of distant friends. With a few good songs and jokes, we parted, with hearty wishes for each other's safety, but this was our last meeting, as nearly all were either killed or badly wounded.

Early in the morning the men were up, getting everything in order, particularly the arms and ammunition. To the doomed town we moved, while the vengeance which each individual denounced against it was awful. We had just entered the trenches below the convent when we met our old General Leith, being carried up wounded, lying on a blanket. He had just joined the Division the day before, after being recovered from his wounds which he received at Salamanca. Some of the men cried out, 'Oh' at this sight, and, 'There's the old General'; others, 'We'll have revenge for that.' In a feeble voice he exclaimed, 'I would not doubt you.' The trenches were now completely filled with troops, eager for the order to advance, while showers of grape came whistling among the bayonets, as we stood waiting for the signal. At length the town clock struck 10, the bugles sounded the advance, and the work of death began. Prior to this all seemed pretty quiet, except for a few guns fired by way of feelers, but now every nerve was strained to enter the place. Without effect the bastion which stood convenient the trench had been mined, and so great was the hurry of the enemy to toss us in the air that they did not let their own men get clear before the explosion took place, and of course sent as many or more of them on an Aerial[22] cruise. The loss of life here was great. I was coming away making use of my firelock as a crutch, having received a grape shot in the right leg when within a few yards of the top of the breach. The scene before me was truly awful. Here you might observe a leg fastened between the ruins of the wall, legs and arms sticking up, some their clothes in flames; numbers not dead, but so jammed as not to be able to extricate themselves, and of course had to remain exposed to the fire of the enemy, which was so thick that you would think it impossible for anything living to escape. Indeed, I never expected to reach my trench with my life, for not content with depriving me of my limb, the fire shot away my crutch also. I was getting on pretty well, the sand being driven in my eyes with the balls and . . . placed my foot on a Portuguese officer, whom I concluded was dead. However, he was so jammed in the ruins of the mine he was obliged to remain there as quiet as possible. When raising his head he cries 'Craho', or 'Damn you'. I paid more attention to scrambling into the trench than to give any heed to his nonesense. Contrary to my expectations, I gained the trench, which was a dismal sight. It was literally filled or rather crammed with the dead and dying. 'Twas lamentable to see the poor fellows here. One was making the best of his way minus an arm; another his face so disfigured and covered with blood as to leave no trace of the features of a human being; others creeping along with the leg dangling to a piece of skin; and worse than all some endeavouring to keep in the bowels. Yet in the midst of this carnage the only note that sounded on the ear was the advance.

Many brave and desperate attempts were made to force an entrance. In vain. None that mounted the breach survived. Though the breaches were large, they were also very steep, and from the top to the street the troops had a perpendicular leap of from 15 to 20 feet, and then had to face an enemy ready to salute them with the ball or bayonet. After spending a considerable time in these fruitless efforts, General Graham ordered our batteries to open on the curtain[23], and so elegantly and accurately was their fire given that the enemy was destroyed. Though the shot could not be more than a few feet over the men, at the same time the Portuguese troops were fording the river from the passage side, exposed to a murderous fire from the castle, which did dismal execution, as we could see the poor fellows carried away by the tide in great numbers. Yet despite every obstacle they gained their point and made a successful attack on the smaller breach on the extreme left. The sailors and marines at the same time had manned a great number of boats from the shipping, and made for the rear of the castle. But this show was a feint to draw the enemy's attention from us. For as soon as they came within range of the guns a full stop took place and left us to finish our own job.

Having reached an old house where the Doctors were at work preparing for Chelsea[24], I got under one of their hands, but an officer coming in, the doctor left me to attend him, when I exclaimed, 'Fair soldiering, Doctor, I'm in first,' on which he returned to me and completed his job. 'Twas here the doctors had fine practice, and most expert they were in leaving a poor fellow minus a wing. This house got completely filled, the upper rooms being the most airy. I had the good fortune to get the breadth of myself on an old floor. It happened that all the old files who had the use of their limbs took it into their heads not to suffer anyone to have access to the room, except those who had suffered the privations of the campaign. Thus we were a chosen few of early boys. A few days after the town had been taken, a number of our comrades got permission to visit those in hospital. And indeed they did not forget us in the money way. Doubloons and dollars were lying on the floor under our pillow (that is to say the knapsack) without count, as had all things in common. Among the rest an old schoolfellow paid me a visit one day, and after handing me a fistful of whatever came first to hand, wheeling round the haversack, which contained 23 watches, desired me to take my pick. Thus you may form some idea of how matters went.

As he sat beside me, he informed me that, on the town being cleared of the French, the work of plunder commenced. 'One of the 95th and I,' says he, 'had agreed to stick together and divide the booty. The first house we entered, the lower part was nearly bare, so upstairs we darted, but a door that was locked stood proof against the butt of the firelock. But having recourse to the soldier's key' – that is fire through the keyhole – 'open flew the door. On the floor lay an old man, a woman and a young man, all dead, from the ball through the keyhole. On which we went away without touching a single article.' It appears they had been looking through the keyhole over each other's shoulders when he unlocked the door with the ball which deprived them of life.

A comrade Sergeant was sitting beside me the same day. 'Well Jim,' said I, 'How did you get into the town at last?' 'Damn me,' said he, 'but we fairly battered them from underneath the back of the breach with stones and brick bats, until we got room to leap down.' The town having been taken, the old trade of plunder and drunkenness commenced. Fires lighted on the boarded floors soon communicated with the adjoining buildings, and no assistance being given by the drunken soldiers, the whole town was nearly reduced to ashes while the plunder carried on board the shipping was immense. Even the soldiers' wives scarcely knew what to wear, for grandeur. Those who a few days before had scarcely as much on them as would make a respectable mop were now rigged out with silks and satins of the richest dyes.

The Castle held out until the 8th September, when our batteries opened with such effect that in a few hours the white flag was hung out and the brave defenders of San Sebastian became prisoners of war; 80 officers, 1,736 rank and file, with 93 pieces of ordnance and an immense stock of ammunition was captured.

In Hospital and at the Depot

In our room we had a poor Frenchman with his arm taken out of the socket, and so completely you would really imagine he was born minus that wing. I often thought the French made use of unfair balls[25] during the siege. Such a number of the wounds mortified it was pitiable to see the poor fellows when seized with the lockjaw[26], for which there is rarely a remedy – going about distracted, to think that in a short time go they must, though in good health. One instance occurred (indeed a rare case). A fine young man of the 59th Regiment, finding his lockjaw coming on, and striving to keep the jaws from closing, by placing a piece of bone between his teeth, to no purpose, in a fit of despair struck himself so violent a blow on the jaw that he actually sprang them open. Nor do I know if the like prescription has been applied to any other patient. Afterwards, one night, we all agreed to have a spree. For this it became necessary to secure the orderly man[27], that is gag him with a trifle.[28] With his assistance and a few who had the use of their limbs we procured two camp kettles and a number of canteens of good wine. This you may think was quite sufficient for 18 men, as each camp kettle held 16 quarts, and each canteen 2, After all were rolled in the blanket, we commenced to form our own little party by placing the kettles in the centre of the floor. To a disinterested looker on the sight (even to Cruikshanks[29]) it would have been well worth employing his pencil. Those who were wounded in the head could move about pretty well, and those in the arms too, while others who had got it in the limbs or thighs were obliged to shuffle along on their breech as well as they could, to form a circle. The poor Frenchman, before alluded to, begged hard to be excused, a favour which, according to the rules of hospitality and fair soldiering, could not be granted. Being seated, a pretty group we formed on the floor, and all nearly naked as the only article of dress that decorated the guests was a shirt, and you may rely on it none of the best, or nicest done up. To work we went on the wine, while pipes and tobacco were in such requisition that the place was completely fumigated. All our promises of silence and good order, after a few rounds, began to be infringed upon, and with the consent of all it was agreed that each man should sing a song, and in none of the lowest keys, which alarmed the doctor, who had to remain in a tent in the garden; the house being so crowded that there was scarcely room for the wounded. Throwing his loose cloak round him with his morning slippers, he glides quietly into the room, standing some time as if riveted to the spot, or unable to speak on viewing the scene before him. At length he steps up to the centre and looking into the kettle he exclaims while he seized it, 'Are you all mad? Are you, Mr Corporal', to me, 'I can hear your song above all the others.' The kettle was ordered away. Away it went, to be thrown out of doors, but no juggler could have transported it more quickly and unseen to a place of security. The canteens lying under the knapsacks were unobserved, and of course escaped. He then commenced a long harangue on our improper conduct, concluding with 'Your wounds will burst out afresh, and more likely you will lose your limbs, if not your lives.' Thinking he had destroyed our store, and seeing us deposited in our blankets, he retired, giving strict orders to the man on duty to be watchful lest we should get more liquor and to have a strict look out through the course of the night lest the scoundrels should break out; an order which the poor fellow was incompetent to discharge, being as full as an egg himself.

Fortunately, I awoke some time through the night, when to my surprise I saw that the wounds of the man on my right had broken out. He was in a profound sleep; a little longer and he would have slept, or would have slipped, into the invisible world. I bawled out so loud that our orderly man came, and clapping on a tourniquet stopped the discharge just in time, as he was nearly off. The weather being uncommonly warm, and the number of wounded so great ... we could not get dressed as often as necessary, so that out of some of the wounds great long-tailed maggots would be tumbling about the floor, and these wounds were considered the most wholesome, as these customers lived on the corrupted flesh which, if left alone, would have turned to mortification. Still it must be admitted they were none of the most desirable companions. A host of hospital mates[30] now swarmed over us to get a lesson in preparing men for Chelsea, two of whom were attached to our regiment, but the poor fellows knew no more than pull off a piece of sticking plaster and clap on another. My comrade, of the name of Traynor from Belfast, seemed rather unfortunate, having received at Corunna a ball about two inches from the left shoulder; and about two inches below it received another at Salamanca. To complete the job he received the third on the breach of San Sebastian about 2 inches lower still, which fractured his arm to the socket. However, the doctor left him a stump, presentable and no more. I had become pretty handy in dressing the wounds, and this poor fellow would suffer no one but me to dress and bandage him, and I really think he would have sunk under it but for the manner in which I endeavoured to keep up his spirits.

After the surrender of the castle the wounded were sent by sea to Bilbao and St Andro (or Santander), the latter being my destination in a wooden house.[31] These houses were made in England; the several parts being numbered, so that the erection of them occupied a very short time. They were both clean and comfortable in good weather, but in wet or cold weather just the reverse. It is a fact undeniable that the wounds received at San Sebastian were longer in healing than those received elsewhere, and more limbs lost. The wound I received mortified in common with many others ... I shall quote the remedy applied. This was a poultice compounded of brown sugar, lees of wine and linseed meal. For my part I actually thought the limb was being dragged off me, but in the morning, on the removal of the poultice, the limb had the appearance of being dipped in tar, the mortified flesh falling off in black streams. The swelling having subsided, the doctors were for making an exchange of limbs, that is taking off the bad one and presenting me with a timber one instead, but I refused my consent, saying, 'If I am to go the limb shall go with me.' This so displeased the General Doctor[32] that he did not pay me a visit for two days afterwards, and then observing the change for the better, he says, 'Well my man, you'll save your limb yet.'

Along with a number of others I got invalided and sent to Passages to wait for conveyance to England. This was the most murderous place I ever came across, or even read of. If any British subject would be foolhardy enough to venture out after night, 'twas next to a miracle if he escaped being stabbed. Almost every morning brought with it fresh proofs of villainy, as the bodies would be found in the streets, and floating in the tide. To relate what I have seen of this kind of Spanish generosity would swell the catalogue of crimes, some of as deep a dye as those committed on the defenceless Mexicans.[33]

Bullfights are a principal amusement in Spain, and here in the main street we were entertained with an exhibition of this sort, but the unfortunate man who engaged the bull got tossed in the air with his entrails round the animal's horns. The Spaniards at this got enraged, and commenced an attack on the poor maimed British, and among others struck an officer. Word soon came to the depot, and there was a show of cripples turned out that was fit to carry a firelock mustered in the square. They formed line, primed and loaded, while the *Kangaroo* sloop of war, which was guard ship, slipped her cable and ran alongside the square, gun ports open and guns run out ready for action. These preparations had a powerful effect on these midnight assassins, who retired before a few wounded British and took shelter in the castle.

Being able to move about with the help of a stick, I was placed as sentinel at the hospital door, having a good chair to rest on with a carbine, and plenty of powder and shot. My employment was to shoot the rats, as the dead house was on the same floor, separated by a slight partition. A large beam that ran across was their route in visiting this depository of the dead, which seldom contained less than half-a-dozen. 'Twas shocking to see them in the morning, with their faces and breasts torn. These midnight assassins were in troops and fine sport I had despatching them by day, but at night there was no remedy.

At length I got round so far as to be sent to the depot, doing duty once more. The main street was chequered half English and half Spanish. I being on the Provost guard, we had to patrol the streets occasionally during the night, with strict orders to take up every British subject that came our way and keep them in the guardhouse until morning, by way of saving their bacon, or in other words to save them from being murdered. In our rambles we happened upon the Master-of-Arms[34] belonging to the *Kangaroo*, and he rather more than half seas over took him up into the guardhouse. At this treatment he was (and justly too) indignant, he being an officer, at least what is termed a Warrant Officer, and to be treated as a private soldier was lessening his consequence. Yet on the other hand we were to be exonerated, as we could afford him no better accommodation, and an imperative duty and order to save his life if possible. On being ushered into this depot of rats, he raged and stormed. 'Was that fit usage for a British officer and a British sailor?' making use of language very unbecoming of a gentleman, and kicking up such a row that no person on guard could sleep, even if the rats (with which the place was swarming) were so inclined. At length, my small stock of patience being totally exhausted, I gave him to understand that if he did not keep a more civil tongue in his head I would gag him, and if that had not the desired effect I would stuff him into the black hole along with 3 men under sentence of death for the robbery of General Castanos in the town of Arnany, and there let the rats eat him. All threatening was of no avail. He still kept on till at last into the condemned cell he was popped, but no stomach pump could have brought him so quickly to his senses. In about an hour he begged and entreated to be liberated from among these midnight marauders, promising most faithfully to conduct himself well for the remainder of the night.

Being liberated, I gave him a blanket to take a nap, but no; so pulling out some money he wanted a refreshment in the shape of more liquor, but in this he was foiled. In a little time he began to reason with me on the impropriety of making him a prisoner. 'No,' said I, 'you are no prisoner, but an intruder on our hospitality, and as soon as you have good daylight you may go where you please, and now let me tell you, I would serve your Admiral the same way if I found him in the streets after hours, circumstanced as you were.'

When day arrived it ushered in the Provost, making enquiries how we stood during the night, to whom this would-be officer lodged many and grievous complaints, of my having made him a prisoner, etc. The Provost, calling me aside, says, 'I'm afraid you have brought yourself into trouble. Did you not know he was an officer?' 'Yes, but your orders specified every British subject, and had I have left him in the streets and he to have been murdered, you would not have come forward to say that officers were exempt.' This closed his mouth. Not so with Mr officer, who threatened to report me to his commander. 'Stop, my friend,' cried I. 'As soon as I get relieved and rubbed up a little you may expect me on board the *Kangaroo*, and I shall inform the Admiral of the whole affair.' This was an attack he was not prepared to repel, and it was not even dreamt of. Calling the Provost he begged of him to use his influence to prevent my making the report as he was quite certain, if I had done so, he would be dismissed the service. So turning the thing over in my mind as a bit of a spree I promised not to make my report, on which, through the Provost, he begged me to accept a guinea for my trouble and the loan of my blanket. Thus I left him to finish his cruise.

By Sea to Gravesend

Along with a great many more from different regiments, I was sent by sea up the Garonne as far as Pollyhack, from which place we sailed for England, under convoy of a frigate. The scenery along the Garonne cannot be exceeded for beauty. From the banks of the river as far as the eye can take in on each side, rising in amphitheatre-like form, it is so interspersed with well-laid-out fields and plantations that it would seem as if each occupant on the very numerous farms vied with each other as to whose dwelling should be most comfortable, and attract the greater notice. Often have I, while smoking my pipe on deck, cast a glance over the beautiful expanse, and turning over in my mind the outward beauty, pictured to myself that, though so fair to look upon, no doubt many of the whitewashed walls contained the venerable remains of sorrowing parents over the earthly loss of a dear child, fallen perhaps in battle, over whose remains the page of history alone can tell the fatal spot on which he fell, in defence of his country, never to return to these happy, or more properly speaking beautiful abodes, though now the olive branch waved throughout the land. At the mouth of the Garonne stands one of the finest lighthouses I have seen.

At some distance out to sea, the old transport in which we were, being manned by none of the best sailors, was the occasion of delaying the fleet very much. One night the weather became very much clouded, and there were signs of an approaching squall, while all the signals of our Commodore proved unavailing to make her mind her pace. Being off the Eddystone, which is none of the most desirable of sea berths, he runs alongside, calling our Captain everything but a gentleman, and swearing in no measured terms, that only on account of the old soldiers he had on board, he would not send him to the bottom. After all his nonsense, we reached Portsmouth in safety, landed and got lodged in Hasler Barrack. From thence, along with about 40 others from 30 different regiments, we marched to Gravesend, or Tilbury Fort, *en route* for Scotland, a Sergeant of the 42nd being senior in charge of the party and subsistence. On the third day's march, or straggle, a group had sat down on the side of the road, refreshing themselves with a puff of the pipe, while some in the rear were making the best way they could . . . and had far to go when a gentleman (seemingly) popped his head out of a coach that was passing, inquiring where we were going, who had charge of the party, with a great many such-like questions. After obtaining the information he required, he then commenced an abusive harangue on our unsoldierlike conduct, and as a finish stroke threatened to report us to the Secretary of War. One of the 87th, rising up and looking him sternly in the face, says, 'If you had done your duty so strictly at Malaga, you would not be here this day, but it is always so with cowards.'[35] This discourse appeared to be long enough, as the whip went to work on the horses, and without having the civility to wish us good morning, he was soon out of sight and hearing. But I suppose he forgot to make his report, as we heard no further of the matter.

We all reached Gravesend in safety, and slipped over to Tilbury Fort, waiting a few days for conveyance to Leith in a smack which was to call for us on her way from London. These were smart little craft, and in time of war carry guns by way of self defence. We now mustered 27 of different regiments stowed away in this article. The old captain behaved to us as well as circumstances would admit of, letting us have beer as long as it lasted (that is for money), but the sunburnt lips of these old campaigners were dry, so that his beer barrels were as empty as a drum in a little time. In the hold lay a great quantity of long rods split for the purpose of making hoops. The hold concealed a few casks of Burton ale, but the prying eyes of the soldier must see to the bottom, so something like the French at the Barrier gates[36] while searching for contraband goods, with long iron rods they commenced to sound the cargo with their bayonets, and soon discovered the concealed treasure. Every article capable of holding liquor was now put in requisition. The Captain was surprised to see the men getting intoxicated, and suspecting all was not right, made a brief visit to the hold, but seeing his intended hoops in proper order, he did not deem it prudent to remove them, lest Mr Burton should be discovered, and then if he had the eyes of Argus,[37] his Burton would soon have disappeared.

We arrived in Leith after a fine passage of three days and as many nights. You may easily judge of the old skipper's consternation on discovering his loss, being minus one and a half casks. For a while he indulged in the greatest passion, but what was to be done? The liquor was gone, and no money forthcoming. At length he got calm and laughed heartily. However, we came to an agreement to make up the money and remit it to him, a proposal which he rejected; he wishing us every success, we parted.

I Rejoin 3rd Battalion
I now joined the 4th Battalion, quartered in Edinburgh Castle, from whence I was ordered to Pennycuic to do duty over a number of French prisoners, left there after the main body had departed. At length a draft was ordered to join the 3rd Battalion. Thus once

more I joined the old fighting comrades in Fermoy. We sailed in a schooner and 2 brigs for old Ireland, but through adverse winds we put into Plymouth, and lay there 3 weeks windbound. At length we were favoured with a fair gale, and away we went for Cork. We had scarcely cleared the harbour when it commenced to blow a storm, so that, as a result of the lashing, the main boom giving way, struck a poor sailor on the head. One of the brigs in company was sculling away under close-reefed foresail about sunset, when one of the men went on deck to light his pipe. The vessel gave a roll and he staggering against the gangway. It flew open and out he went. He swam well for some time, but having on the great coat it prevented his exertions, calling for help, which the captain refused, saying he would not endanger the loss of all for one man. Thus the poor man perished. The storm continued to increase. Our Captain, to shun the Silly rocks[38], stood out to sea. When he was about to nail down the hatches, I sprung out on deck without shoe or stocking. For two days and nights, through frost and snow, I ran the deck, drenched to the skin, while our foremast and bowsprit were carried away.

Thus, like an old tub we rolled into Kinsale harbour, on Christmas eve 1814. In the course of a few days we proceeded for Cork, from thence to Fermoy, where we lay during the winter. In Fermoy we were very comfortable, too much so to last long.

Chapter Six

The Waterloo Campaign

Although Pamplona did not finally fall to Wellington until 31 October, 1813, his troops had already crossed the Bidassoa on the 7th and so were now on French soil. As Napoleon was being defeated in Germany at Leipzig, in the Battle of the Nations, and was about to begin his fighting withdrawal that would end outside Paris, Wellington began his advance towards Bayonne, which would continue to hold out gallantly for some months. He was vigorously resisted by Soult who, despite being defeated on the Nive and at St Pierre, refused to give up the struggle, even when he learned in Toulouse of Napoleon's abdication on 6 April, 1814. However, after another hard fight, Toulouse fell on the 11th, Soult having managed to withdraw to the south. Despite a most determined sortie by the garrison, which took the British by surprise and almost spelled disaster for them, Bayonne capitulated on the 27th and the last shots of the Peninsular War had been fired.

The bulk of Wellington's veterans were now sent to America to take part in the closing stages of the war of 1812. Napoleon was sent in exile to Elba from where he escaped in March, 1815. Given a rapturous welcome on his return to France, he soon gathered a substantial army of his old troops around him, including the bulk of his beloved Old Guard. Louis XVIII had fled the country and Napoleon was once again its de facto ruler.

As soon as the news of Napoleon's escape reached the capitals of the Allies, Wellington was sent from London to assume command of the Anglo-Dutch and Allied armies in Belgium. This was a motley force of some 90,000 men, of whom 30,000 were British. Even they were mostly untried troops. Wellington would later describe his new command as the worst army, with the worst equipment and the worst staff, that he had ever commanded. Meanwhile, field Marshal Blücher and a Prussian army of some 120,000 men, of whom more than half were raw recruits or militiamen, was advancing from the Rhineland to come to Wellington's support. By this time Napoleon had deployed one of the best armies he ever commanded, in terms of experience and quality, composed mainly of veterans who had been released from captivity at the end of the war, including a strong Imperial Guard. Aware of Blücher's approach, he determined to drive a wedge between him and Wellington and to defeat his two opponents in detail.

He now attacked the Prussians at Ligny. Despite Wellington's advice, which was rejected, Blücher had unwisely deployed on a forward slope and was soundly beaten for his pains, being badly hurt himself in the battle when his horse was shot under him. By good fortune, a muddle between Marshal Ney and D'Erlon, one of his corps commanders, prevented Napoleon from outflanking Blücher and Ney had now to switch his attack to Quatre Bras where a weak Dutch-Belgian force was sited but was already begining to be reinforced by the British, who had to be thrown piecemeal into the battle to check the French advance. This they succeeded in doing, but at a heavy price in lives lost. Thanks to an inexplicable delay by Napoleon in issuing fresh orders, Wellington was able to slip away under cover of a cavalry rearguard action to reach his chosen ground of Mont St Jean, on the road to Brussels, during the evening of 17 June.

The Battle of Waterloo, which began on the following morning, was a titanic struggle which ebbed to and fro all day. Thanks in no small part to the brave old Blücher, who was determined to come to the aid of his allies, in spite of the battering his army had suffered at Ligny and who now advanced across terrible roads and rain-soaked fields to threaten Napoleon's right flank, the day was saved. As soon as he realized that the Prussians were at hand and forcing Napoleon to turn his attention to that flank, Wellington launched his counter-attack with devastating effect. By last light it was all over. For the first time in its history, the Guard had broken and the whole French army, headed by their Emperor, was in headlong flight. As Wellington was so famously to observe, it had been a close-run thing.

With Napoleon once more in exile, the Allies established an Army of Occupation in France and the 3rd Battalion The Royal

Scots remained outside Paris until March, 1817, when they were sent home to England and disbanded at Canterbury on 24 April.

*   *   *

Early in the month of April, being in town one evening, the mail coach passing through had a large placard fastened to the boot, on which was printed in large characters, that no mistake might occur, 'Bonaparte's escape from Elba'. On reading this, off I started for the barracks. 'Come my boys, you may be getting your knapsacks in order.' To the general inquiry of 'What's up now?' I replied, 'Why our old friend has got loose again.' Having made his escape, every wheel was now in motion to get things in proper order. Though we had no notice, it was more than likely we would be on the move ere long. Accordingly, we were inspected by General Forbes, who expressed himself highly pleased with the appearance and high state of discipline of the men. The same evening we were served out with a little ballast in the shape of 60 rounds per man. This served as a preface to another campaign. Camp kettles, billhooks, etc, were issued and we were bound for the route for Cork. On May 1st, 1815, we marched with the old tune of 'The girl I left behind me.' We remained here 5 days. On the 6th May we marched for Cove. A few minutes before leaving the barracks, Col Campbell[1] enlisted a young man and brought him along; but as we had no spare clothing, arms and accoutrements, he was obliged to wear his own regimentals, and was actually brought onto the field at Quatre Bras, where he received a ball through the hand, was sent home with a shilling a day for life, and never pulled a trigger, or wore a red coat in the service. This is one instance of blind fortune, while others who to my knowledge went through all the hardships of the Peninsular War got rewarded with a blank discharge.[2]

I shall now give you a say on surgery. A corporal of our company of the name of Olday had received a ball in the knee at Vitoria, which fractured the bone to such a degree that he had carefully laid up 54 pieces of bone which came out of the wound; notwithstanding, it healed up and with a very slight halt he was enabled to do his duty. But the passage from Cove to the Downs caused it to break out afresh, and it now wore the appearance of life or limb. Still the doctor would not operate on him, as the ball had damaged the joint. We had a drunken old file of the name of Frazer, a hospital orderly, whose business it was to attend the doctor and assist in dressing wounds, and serve out to the patients the prescriptions. This old customer proposed to Olday to extract the ball. He consented, and to work he went. Making an incision as deep as he possibly could, he extracted the ball, flattened in parts as thin as tin, and in several pieces. To complete the job, he sucked the wound clear of bones and lead, spitting out the blood and matter. Then, the wound being dressed, Olday recovered so fast as to be able to do duty in a fortnight's time. But on the morning of 18th June he received another ball a little below the old one, after which I never saw him more.

We sailed from Cove for the Downs, where we remained just as long as to shift from one vessel to another, and away for Ostend. On arriving there we piled arms in a large piece of waste ground on the right of the town. Bales of blankets were opened, and each man served out with one, and in a good many cases more than that complement. As the old Dutch frows[3] were serving out the Schnappes at such a rate, and at the same time were not idle in swathing themselves under the hoop petticoats, in this manner a great number were carried off unnoticed. We halted for a little while on the banks of the canal, waiting for boats. Here we got highly entertained in a garden very tastefully laid out with seats and arbours. The landlord of the inn pocketed the gilt in great style, while all distinction was levelled as the gin began to operate. Officers and men were all alike, while the songs went round in full chorus.

The bugles called us reluctantly away, and into the boats we scrambled, and away for Ghent by Bruges. We were quartered in the first mentioned place for some time, living in splendour with lots of green forage[5] for supper. During our sojourn here a draft from our 4th Battalion joined. The adjutant announced their arrival to the Colonel, who inquired how many there were. 'Forty,' said the adjutant. 'Forty thieves,' cried the Colonel, and by that appellation they were known as long as a man of them remained in the ranks. From Ghent we marched to Brussels. Here we enjoyed ease and plenty. We had a drummer of the name of Duffey, no favourite of the adjutant's, and indeed anything lighter than a sheet anchor would not be safe in his charge. One day he resorted to a rather curious as well as a dangerous shift. He starts off to his Grace's valet, with a message as if from Col Campbell, who desired that a suit of livery might be sent to him for the purpose of having a suit made for his servant of the same pattern. The unsuspecting valet sends one of his best suits, which in a short time changed masters, while Duffey pocketed the guilders. The servant, finding that the goods were not returned according to promise, began to make some inquiry, and to his loss had to add the mortification of being duped by a drummer. In the meantime Duffey was confined and warned for a court martial. The court assembled and Serjeant Connor sent for the prisoner. On coming to the guard room, the Serjeant of the guard was sending a Corporal and a file of the guard, but looking at the prisoner O'Connor exclaims it would be a shame to send a guard with such a thing as that. 'Come along,' he said, and off they went. But the first turn they came to Duffey made a start, Connor after, but to no purpose, as he was soon out of sight. And poor Connor, after searching in vain for upwards of two hours, returned to the court to report his own misconduct and the loss of his prisoner and was reduced to the rank and pay of a private. But at Quatre Bras, being ordered by the Colonel to go to the rear and bring up some ammunition, he received a ball in the buttock on which he sang out, 'What the devil would I care, but to be hit in so disgraceful a place.' The Colonel, overhearing the remark, cried out, 'Make that fellow Sergeant again.' thus, if he was disgracefully wounded, which could not be denied, he was honourably restored to his former rank.

Quatre Bras

We lived in ease till the 15th June, when a few waggon loads of wounded Prussians[6] arrived, which was the first signal we had of the work being begun. That night, we were as usual comfortable, and a great deal more so, as the Duchess of Richmond had given a ball to the officers of the garrison, when a little after midnight the bugles went to work in all directions, and the ball broke up; each regiment retired to their respective alarm posts and in a few hours, all being in readiness, rations served out. To the road we went for Quatre Bras.

We had about 20 miles to march and halted for the purpose of cooking, when a straggling shell coming over the camp told us in language not to be mistaken that the enemy were not far off. In a few minutes the cooking was settled with the utensils packed up and the guests preparing for another kind of entertainment. We were ordered 'Stand to your arms', fell in, the ammunition examined, flints fast.[7] All's right. Here we moved forward a little, filed to the right into a field of rye as tall as our grenadiers, and the play began.

We were rather awkwardly placed, not being able to destroy the enemy until close at hand. Their cavalry being numerous, whereas we had none, we were obliged to form square against cavalry, and after sending them to the four winds, form line against infantry. Thus for want of cavalry we were kept forming squares and lines from between 2 and 3 o'clock in the afternoon until dark. When in square they plied us tight with round shot, and in line with grape, so that the rye was prematurely cut down by an invisible hand, as between the 2 fires and the trampling of men and horses it was laid low in a short time. In one charge of the cuirassiers[8], we were so short taken, not being aware of the advance of the cavalry, that the 28th Regiment and we had to form one square, with Picton[9] in the centre. On came the Lancers full charge but the murderous fire they received swept them off their saddles in great style. Thus they persevered in breaking the square, making a trial at each face, until very few of them were left to carry the intelligence to their comrades. On the defeat of the Cavalry, Sir Thomas Picton returned thanks to the two regiments[10], saying he could not desire it better done (and it must be allowed he was a pretty well experienced judge in such matters), adding that he would recommend them to the Government to wear feathers[11], but he fell on the 18th of June and with him fell the feathers.

The enemy being defeated on every point left us in possession of this well disputed field for the night. Nor did they seem inclined to renew a 2nd trial in the morning. Removing the wounded as well as circumstances would admit gave ample employment for a time, when about 10 or 11 o'clock we commenced to fall back through Genappe, and so on towards Waterloo.

Waterloo
The cavalry joining fast, the rain descending in torrents rendered the roads most miserable. Of course the enemy were in no better circumstances, in hopes no doubt we were making for our only refuge, the wooden walls.[12] But if they entertained such an idea they were miserably deceived. For about 7 in the evening we got into our position drenched to the skin, without a spot that we could stretch our wearied frames upon unless in mud. Yet the enemy were not content in letting us enjoy this luxury, but commenced to drive us on. But finding us a little obstinate in our determination to keep our berth, they gave over and left us in this stubborn temper to enjoy our repose.

The morning of the 18th was ushered in, both armies drawn up in order of battle, and viewing each other with a determination not to yield up their former hard-earned labours. The French no doubt were confident of success, having the conqueror of Lodi, Marengo and Austerlitz to dwarf them, and their ranks filled up with old veterans from the hulks[13] now turned to revenge the former defeat; whilst the British, equally confident of Wellington, stood cleaning out their pieces, preparing their ammunition, and getting all things in order for the conflict which was to decide the fate of Europe and write on the page of history, to be transmitted to the latest posterity, the word 'Waterloo'.

Had the number of troops which Wellington commanded all been British, the contest would not have lasted so long, nor would the French have left the field with so large a fragment as did escape the army. But he had to trust to the Belgians[14] and others, in places where they very early in the day showed the seam of their stocking to the enemy. Their first attempt was brave, had it been followed up, for as the French advanced to attack La Haye Sainte, they boldly advanced to meet them with the bayonet. But seeing the French stand their ground, to the rightabout they went, and running 'manfully' through our ranks caused some confusion. Here we had to supply their place by leaping over a low hedge and then powering in a well-directed volley. The whole of the French brigade were made prisoner.

The action had now commenced in great style. The thunder of such a number of cannon was tremendous, while masses of cavalry rushing forward to force the adamantine squares fell in heaps beneath the British fire. Though their pigeon-breasted armour was of use if struck in a slanting position, where the well-rammed ball struck fair, through it went. Our squares at the commencement of the action were placed on the face of the hill and were completely exposed to the shot of the enemy, which did great execution. Wellington, to remedy this, retired us a little over the crest of the hill, which caused the guns to be in advance while we were less exposed during the repeated charges of cavalry.[15] The artillerymen had often to take shelter in the squares, while some lay under the guns to save themselves from the Lancers. In one of these attacks the French attacked with masses of infantry, cavalry, and a numerous train of artillery to force the centre.

Here brave Picton advanced the Division 4 deep to oppose them, but on coming to a close encounter with a bayonet, they fired a volley, but Picton fell.[16] The slaughter was great on both

99

sides, and would have been greater, but for the ground, which, being so soft, the balls which struck it never rose again. Thus we were kept the whole day repelling their attacks, exposed to a murderous cannonade, and musketry from the farm house of La Haye Sainte. The last attempt to force the centre in the evening was 'Do or die'. Wellington and his staff came galloping up the hill, swords drawn. On reaching the squares he says, 'Here comes the cavalry, don't be alarmed.' then, dashing into one of the squares, awaited the onset.

The fire from the guns had for some time been slacker than usual, owing to the ammunition getting scarce, while that of the enemy seemed to increase. On dashed the cavalry, and in despite of the grape crowned the hill, and kept dancing among the squares, while nearly 40 pieces of cannon were at their command.[17] This, in my opinion, was the crisis of the battle. If they had had the means of getting them away the French would have gained the field. This was entirely out of their power, and to remain in this way for any length of time would not do, as the squares were mowing them down in great style. So, giving up the contest, they abandoned the hill.

In the midst of this crisis Quartermaster Griffiths, whose proper place was with the baggage in the rear, hearing of our last officer, Brigade Major McDonald, being badly wounded[18], came galloping into the square. 'Griffiths,' cries McDonald, 'you must take the command.' 'Yes,' says he, drawing his sword, 'two years ago I was Private in the Royals and now I command the 3rd Battalion in the field.'[19] McDonald, sitting on horseback was addressed by Griffiths, dismounted, who says, 'McDonald, you'll be killed.' 'Never heed,' was the cool reply, 'a ball will kill me on foot as will one on horseback.'[20]

A supply of ammunition now arrived and, though late, came up in force. The British so long on the defensive were impatient for close quarters, longing and even calling out for the order to advance, eager to put an end to this glorious day of destruction, in which the patience, bravery and fortitude of the British soldier was put to the utmost trial. Four deep we advanced with 3 British cheers, while the sun, hitherto obscured, now shone forth, as if smiling on the last efforts of Britain for the liberties of Europe. We were supported by the cavalry, while the enemy gave way in the utmost confusion, abandoning their guns, and everything they possessed. The Prussians, coming up at the critical moment, struck up, as we met at La Belle Alliance[21] the national air of 'God save the King'.

Thus ended the battle of Waterloo, as far as the fighting part concerned the British.

And on to Paris

The moon now shone forth in silent silvery splendour, giving the Prussians an opportunity of revenging the disastrous results of Jena, which was distinctly heard through the greater part of the night, by the distant sound of cannon fired by these unwearied pursuers. We halted that night on the position occupied by the enemy during the day. The Commissary arrived with the ration liquor, and out of a company 100 strong, on the morning of the 19th eleven sat around to drink, not the health but the memory of those who had vacated their places in the ranks, some numbered with the dead, others – and not a few – who, being badly wounded, never survived. And again, others, though they survived, yet being unfit for service, were sent away with a solitary 6d or 9d, to drag out a miserable life on a ticket[22], while in many instances those poor fellows with bad wounds and broken constitutions have been refused employment – if capable of earning a little – because they were liberally rewarded by their generous country. It may be considered and said to be a false statement, but I know it be the fact again, that others have I seen enjoying large pensions who have never burned powder against the enemy. What would be said by a poor fellow, with 2 musket balls lodged in him and 3 bayonet wounds, getting rewarded with a blank discharge to exhibit to his offspring, and say, 'I was once a soldier, but because these wounds did not occasion the loss of a limb, or disable me from earning my bread, I was not considered a fit subject to be rewarded with a trifle to keep me from begging, having spent the flower of my days in defence of my generous country.' Is this an exaggerated statement? No! But too true.

On the 20th we commenced our march or pursuit by way of Malplaquet, Cato[23] and so on towards Paris, and encamped at Clichy, on the banks of the Seine, about two miles from that city on the 26th of June, the barrier at Clichy being pretty well secured by some 9 pounders, and a strong guard, no private soldier being allowed to enter without a pass signed by his Commanding Officer. Several of our officers, however, were quartered in the city, which during the fine weather was a little recreation for

them, but was rather troublesome to the non-commissioned officers, if any orders were issued which affected them. Not that I can say we were at all times displeased with the job of showing them.[24]

One night a Sergeant of the 95th and I, after having shown our orders, adjourned into a grand cafe to regale ourselves, as well as to take shelter from a heavy shower coming on. Not willing to intrude without a recompense[25], we drank pretty freely. At length to the road we went, as wet inside as out, when outside the barrier, some ladies and gentlemen were sauntering about. One of the gents made inquiry where we were going, it being after hours. A person wearing a coloured coat, making himself so officious in soldiers' concerns, rather irritated us and to his astonishment, he received for answer, 'Ask our A—'. Upon this he sung out most lustily for the guard, a number of which turned out. But, you may rest assured, there was not much dirt stuck to heels. The men pursued, but not with the intention of capturing us, so after about half a mile of a run we halted. All's right, having escaped the fangs of our pursuers. We jogged on, and down came the rain again, which the large trees on each side of the road kept off for a time, when up drives a carriage. We demanded admittance, but was stoutly refused, as it contained an old French gentleman. Seizing the reins, I then put one foot on the spoke of the wheel to ascend, when the driver gives the animals the whip. My leg got entangled in the wheel, and away I went, quick as steam. On the road I lay unable to move. My comrade dragged me into shelter and started to look for the orderly book[26], which was lost in the scuffle, but could not be found. In a little time I recovered and we resumed our march toward the camp, wet and dirty minus the orderly book. The night proved very wet and early in the morning a pizzano offered the book for sale to a comrade Sergeant, who paid him with threatening him with the General, but it was swelled three times its ordinary size with the wet. Perhaps you are curious to know who the Gent was who sung out for the guard, and I dare say will be a little surprised to hear of no less a personage than Lord Castlereagh.[27]

In the Army of Occupation
We remained in this camp till the 29th October and marched for winter cantonments to Maule, Montmorency, Gillecourt and adjacent villages. We joined the garrison at Valenciennes in January 1816, forming part of the 6th Division of the army of

occupation, under the command of Sir Charles Colville. We remained in this garrison until the month of October, when a grand review[28] took place on the plains of Denain, between Valenciennes and Bouchain. The 21st was the date fixed for this giant exhibition. The morning proved uncommonly fine, so that we expected to have great sport. After being inspected by his Grace, we moved off and made an attempt at Bouchain, but were forced to retire. The attack on this garrison was the principal object of this day's work. In our first attempt we were repulsed, and retired through a swamp, when to give the thing an air of reality the place over which we were retiring was laid under water, in places knee deep. Through this we plodded, until we got on terra firma, and then marching by a circuitous route got in an opposite direction from where the first attempt was made. The rain now descended in torrents, and the sport was spoiled, night coming on. Each regiment commenced to find the nearest way to their respective camps. 'Twas really laughable to see the fire of musketry which would be opened when they arrived at a ditch that they might see where to leap.[29] The stragglers were numerous and numbers did not reach the camp until morning. The main body got in about 2 am, hungry, wet and weary. Numbers of the guns were not extricated from the swamp until several days later.

The town of Bouchain is small, and on the road from Paris is not seen until close upon it, when a sharp turn of the road brings you in full view of this little Gibraltar and within a few perches[30] of its barrier. This town being the last exploit of the great Marlborough, I could not restrain my curiosity and turn over in my mind the hero, who in the days of Anne had perhaps trod the spot in which I stood, and in all probability would have marched to Paris had he been supported, as his great deeds and genius deserved, but what will not the tongue of slander accomplish, or endeavour to accomplish? Was Wellington free from its fangs? No. But independent of the enemy in the field the more to be dreaded, subtle enemy in secret was not able to subdue his (I might almost say) more than human fortitude, and perserverance, as he conquered both at home and abroad. Not so with brave Marlborough. Though able in the Cabinet as in the field, yet he found the current of a nation's whims, buoyed up to such a pitch by the prevailing faction of the day, that it was more easy for him to force the lines of Schellenburg or Malplaquet than to bring them to absolve him of his wrongs.[31]

Nothing very material happened while in this garrison, with the exception of one man having been executed for coining[32], one received 900 lashes and one 18 months' solitary confinement, all for the same offence. The French people were greatly attached to the British and I assure you I never spent so pleasant a time during my soldiering. I have seen the old and young shed tears in abundance at our leaving them and numbers of men, being discharged, went back and got married, and are there to this day. We remained in Valenciennes till the 10th March 1817, on which day we marched for Calais, where we arrived on Patrick's eve, and a precious Patrick's day we had, as each man, or nearly so, sold their blankets, to raise the money for the spree. However, the Secretary of War stood to us and made no charge.

Return and disbandment
We embarked for England and landed at Dover on the 24th of the same month. Shortly after we marched for Canterbury and the Battalion was disbanded on 24th April 1817. The Colonel, while reading the order for the disbandment of the battalion, was greatly affected, and several of the old officers tore off pieces of the colours to hold in remembrance of their old campaigns. 'Twas pitiable to see a number of men sent to the 4 winds to begin the world afresh.

Epilogue

Having conducted you through this fighting concern, thankful ought you to be to the Author of all mercies that you have never witnessed the desolating scourges of war, and no less thankful the soldier, who having endured the hardships of the Peninsular War, returned home enriched with a blank discharge. What a field of reflection is the life of a soldier. While sitting at ease, he turns over in his mind that, when called upon to stand in defence of his king and country, what perils, what hardships, what hunger and thirst, what pain and wearings, does he not undergo? Those at home (at least a great number of them) for whose safety and repose he suffers all, to keep them wallowing in luxury, would scarcely afford him (were he or his offspring in want) a night's shift under a roof that they would consider too indifferent an accommodation for his cattle. 'Oh my country,' exclaimed as brave a soldier as ever adorned the British ranks, while we were advancing to the rugged heights of Busaco, when we were overtaken by a tremendous fall of rain, and there we stood to let the water run off as well as possible, while this stern soldier, looking on the hungry drenched beings around him, cries, 'Oh my country, what we suffer for you,' and I believe it was from his heart. And truly might he say so, since from that period often have I heard the same expression made use of by way of mockery or derision.

Now, let us not part without a joke. One morning, while in Canterbury, a comrade Sergeant of the name of Bloxham and I were waiting for the bugle to sound for parade when he spies an elderly woman coming across the square. 'Now,' said he, 'that old woman and I are of one opinion this moment.' 'How could you make that appear?' said I. 'Why, that's the old midwife, and she's just thinking I will never pay her, and I am of the same opinion.'

Bloxham's uncle was one time Lord Mayor of Dublin, and Bloxham was a printer by trade. He was a curious man. If in a hurry for a little grub, he would take his morsel of beef and putting it on a ramrod held it to the fire until done. This he designated a ramrod steak.

The plunder that some men make in action appears to me, or rather plainly presents itself, that he who makes plunder has not done his duty. It is very evident, if a soldier keeps his ranks it is not plunder that will occupy his time. I have had opportunities of enriching myself frequently, and plunder, with the exception of a little grub, never entered my haversack; while others have I seen with more than abundance, and in the end died beggars, while now, thanks be to God, both I and my family are comfortable. To this day I never sit down to meat without the hardships we endured flashing fresh on the memory, and causing a thankfulness to the bountiful creator for having so liberally supplied my wants.

The comparison which I would draw between the British and French soldiers would be thus. The latter at the commencement of an action are all spirit and bravery, but when manfully opposed, or the encounter is of any duration, they relax and finally give way. The former are just the reverse; patient under hardships, not easily roused, but when excited no danger can stop their headlong career. 'Tis either death or victory, and no note on the bugle is so well known as the advance.

IN CONCLUSION

I need not take up my reader's time in relating my joining the veteran battalion, from which I received a handsome pension of 9d per diem, got married, and had it pleased God to have spared all the children, they would have stood at 13 sons and 4 daughters!

FINIS

Chapter Notes

1. Enlistment and My First Campaign

1. Before the advent of the railways the canal system, which had been created in the second half of the 18th Century and by 1809 covered much of the country, was a principal means of transportation.
2. It was all too common for men to be infested with lice when they were enlisted.
3. Blankets kept in hospital for the sole use of those who have the itch. *Author's Footnote.*
4. John Pitt, Second Earl of Chatham and eldest son of William Pitt the Elder. Although a professional soldier, he had served in his younger brother's ministry as First Lord of the Admiralty, Lord Privy Seal and President of the Privy Council. Such dual careers were very common in the 18th and 19th Centuries. John Pitt continued with his military duties, even on active service, whilst still holding his political appointments. A favourite of King George III, to whose patronage he owed much of his advancement, it is commonly thought that he was given command of the Walcheren Expedition to assuage his disappointment when Arthur Wellesley (later Duke of Wellington) was appointed to command the Peninsular Army in 1808.
5. Andrew Hay had commanded the 3rd Royal Scots at Corunna, having assumed command in 1807. Now, at Walcheren, he was commanding a brigade. He was killed in 1814, then a major general, whilst commanding the outposts covering Bayonne.
6. Douglas uses the term 'halberd' here, but it seems likely that he is actually referring to a Sergeant's spontoon – a broad, round-based blade, usually carrying two side spikes and fitted to a long pole. The spontoon replaced the rather ineffective halberd which had been carried by officers. It was issued to NCOs in 1792.

7. The term 'wing' refers to one half of a battalion.
8. Cat-o'-nine tails.
9. Lieutenant General Lord Henry William Paget, eldest son of the Earl of Uxbridge. Having commanded the 7th Hussars with notable success, he distinguished himself in command of a cavalry division under Sir John Moore in the Corunna Campaign. At Walcheren he was commanding an infantry division. He would later achieve immortal fame as the commander of Wellington's cavalry and artillery at Waterloo. Losing a leg in that battle, he was ever after known throughout the Army as 'Old One Leg'. Created Marquess of Anglesey in 1815, he was promoted Field Marshal in 1846.
10. Major General Thomas Graham, commander of a brigade in the 1st Division. Like Hay and Paget, he had served under Moore at Corunna and was, in fact, one of the few who were present at Moore's death and burial. One of Wellington's most successful commanders in the Peninsula, he was created Baron Lynedoch in 1814 and promoted General in 1821.
11. i.e. The light companies, whose principal role was to deal with enemy skirmishers and sharpshooters.
12. 'round and grape'. Roundshot: a solid spherical shot – or cannon ball-fired from a field gun. Grapeshot: also known as 'case' or 'cannister'. It was a close range projectile primarily intended for use during the final stages of an enemy assault. Consisting of a tin case which fitted the bore of the gun or howitzer from which it was fired, it was filled with loose bullets which spread like the shot from a sporting gun and were lethal out to about 500 yards.
13. Lieutenant Donald McLean. The day before we landed he had our Company paraded and addressing them says: 'Now men as many of you as have clean shirts put them on and shave, for God knows but it may be the last.' As he said this he seemed greatly affected, as if some forebodings told him 'Your days are numbered'; and, indeed, not in this case alone but in many have I been witness to men going into action who had been told distinctly they were to fall and so it turned out. *Author's Footnote*
14. The infantryman carried a black leather cartridge pouch behind his right hip, his bayonet and scabbard being behind the left.
15. The Royal Scots, the Regiment being designated The First Royal Regiment of Foot between 1751–1812.
16. The King's German Legion (KGL) had been formed after the Electorate of Hanover had been occupied by the French in 1803, the small Hanoverian Army having been in no position to resist. The Army was subsequently disbanded and the Duke of Cambridge,

who administered the Kingdom on behalf of his father, King George III, conceived a plan to raise a force from the disbanded army for service with the British and submitted it to his Brother, the Duke of York, then Commander-in-Chief of the British Army, who welcomed the idea. The employment of Germans to fight alongside British soldiers was by no means new. A number of excellent German regiments, provided by various small German states for badly needed funds, had served with distinction in America during the American War of Independence.

The original planned strength of the KGL was 4,000. However, recruiting went so well that by the time of the Walcheren Expedition had risen to 14,000. The Duke of Cambridge was its Colonel-in-Chief and responsible for recruitment, appointments and supply. Although recruitment of all European nationalities was allowed, the majority of the troops, now formed into two light and seven line infantry battalions, five cavalry regiments and units of artillery, engineers and supply, were Hanoverians. A number of their officers were British, not least because commissions in the KGL could be had without purchase.

The KGL served later with distinction in the Peninsula, especially at Salamanca and, later still, at Waterloo. In 1812, in recognition of its services, its officers were granted permanent ranks in the British Army.

17. The British Army was equipped with 3,6,9,12 and 24 pr guns, the 6 and 9 prs being those most commonly used. The 24 pr referred to here was effective for breaching defensive works. With round shot it could breach 12 feet of packed earth and was used to great effect in all Wellington's Peninsular sieges.

18. Artillery drivers were members of the Corps of Royal Artillery Drivers, so designated in 1806. It superseded the Driver Corps, the first organization to employ soldiers and army horses, which dated from 1793. Before that date, civilian drivers and hired horses had been employed. Artillery drivers and their horses were allocated to field artillery batteries as required.

19. Designed by Sir William Congreve, the contemporary rocket was first used in action in 1806 when eighteen vessels fired 200 rockets into Boulogne, causing considerable destruction. A year later, no less than 40,000 were fired into Copenhagen. The Mounted Rocket Corps, consisting of two troops and associated with the Royal Horse Artillery, was formed in 1813. A range of different calibres was available including an airburst cannister round. The rockets' extremely erratic behaviour exercised a profound psychological

effect upon the enemy.

Wellington never liked rockets but reluctantly accepted them after the Corps was formed and they were used both in Spain and at Waterloo.

20. Douglas is presumably referring to mortars here (see Note 21).
21. These boats were known as 'bombs'. First used by the French at the end of the 17th Century, they were employed to fire mortar bombs into enemy fortresses and shore defences. Until 1804, the mortars were manned by detachments of the Royal Artillery consisting of a subaltern officer and ten men. On the formation of the Royal Marine Artillery in that year, the responsibility passed to them.
22. The bombardment by naval vessels began at 1300 hours on 13 August, supplementing the fire of fifty-one heavy siege guns already deployed ashore.
23. The French garrison of Flushing numbered between 8–9,000 men. Of these, 5,800 were taken prisoner on the surrender of the town, a further 1,800 having been captured or deserted already. Between 30 July and 17 August British casualties totalled 738 killed, wounded or missing.
24. 4 September, 1346–4 August, 1347.
25. Chatham's troops were endeavouring to navigate the Sloe Channel, which connected the East and West Scheldt. Working off obsolete maps, Chatham had failed to realize that what had been open water in the 17th Century was now obstructed by sandbanks which had been thrown up over the years.
26. This is the first of Douglas's references to the epidemic of what became known as Walcheren fever (see the historical note at the beginning of this chapter on page 3.).
27. On Walcheren.
28. As Douglas himself experienced, the malarial relapses often continued over a period of years.
29. The Society of Friends, whose existence dates from 1652, have a long and distinguished record of social welfare and reform.

2. To War Again: The Battles of Busaco and Sabugal

1. Transportation to a penal colony. A common punishment for even minor infringements of the law, such as petty theft, and an alternative to hanging.
2. The roles of the soldiers' wives on campaign included cooking, washing and foraging, although it was common for them to turn their hands to any device by which they could make money.

However, their devotion to their menfolk and their courage and fortitude were remarkable. At times their suffering, such as the privations of the retreat to Corunna, was terrible and many died, their children also. Yet at such times they would often help to carry the equipment of a sick or wounded soldier and allow him to ride on their donkey. A wife who became widowed was in a desperate plight and almost instant remarriage, to any man that would take her, was all too common.

3. The nickname of the East Norfolk Regiment (9th of Foot). It was acquired in the Peninsula where the Portuguese and Spaniards believed that the regimental badge – the seated figure of Britannia – depicted the Virgin Mary.

4. The River Tagus

5. Presumably Douglas is referring to the rats which must have abounded in such a situation.

6. Later Lieutenant General Sir John Cameron. Commanded the 2nd Battalion The 9th Foot throughout the Peninsular War with great skill and courage and took part in almost all Wellington's major engagements. In his *Peninsular War* (Book xi Ch. 7) William Napier writes in glowing terms of Cameron's leadership at Busaco where the Battalion attacked the élite regiments of Reynier's corps, who had established themselves in the heart of the British position, and put them to flight.

7. Wellington later described the Portuguese as 'the fighting cocks' of his army. Although the Portuguese Army had been in a sorry state in 1808, when Wellington first arrived in the Peninsula to support their country – ill led, badly equipped and administered, with morale at its nadir – and was effectively disbanded in that year, after Junot's invasion, Wellington took very positive steps to correct the situation in 1809. At his request, Major General William Beresford was appointed Marshal of Portugal by the Portuguese Government in the rank of Lieutenant General with a clear brief to put matters to rights. Wellington himself, as Marshal General, was in overall command. Beresford was an extremely able administrator. Having introduced a number of British officers at company level and upwards, he instituted better pay, reasonable food, improved equipment (mostly of British origin) and more equitable discipline. The innate qualities of the Portuguese soldier soon began to emerge. The troops showed themselves to be 'very willing, obedient and patient' and, as Wellington was to imply, very courageous in battle. They now represented an invaluable element of Wellington's force. At Salamanca, in July, 1812, over half the Allied troops were Portu-

guese. In recognition of their services, the whole Army, less one division and the cavalry, was absorbed into the British divisional system, the Portuguese element numbering 28,792 against 52,484 British. In addition to the Army, each of the forty-eight Portuguese regions contributed a regiment to the Territorial Militia, which, although not battleworthy, relieved the regulars of garrison duties and so performed a valuable role.

The contribution made by the Portuguese troops was such that it would have been extremely difficult for the British Army to have won the war without them. Their reputation was such that in 1812 Sir Thomas Picton, one of the greatest divisional commanders in the history of the British Army, and by no means generous in his praise, said of them that beside their British comrades they were 'deserving of an equal portion of the laurel'.

8. Douglas's battalion served in Greville's Brigade in this division.
9. Leith had commanded a brigade under Sir John Moore and joined the Peninsular Army in 1810 as a brigade commander in Sir Rowland Hill's division before taking command of a mixed body of British and Portuguese troops, which then became the 5th Division under his command. Like Douglas, he was a victim of Walcheren fever. He suffered a relapse after the Battle of Busaco which resulted in him being sent home on sick leave. He returned to the Army in January, 1812, after the fall of Ciudad Rodrigo. Promoted to Lieutenant General in the following year, he was wounded two days before the final assault on San Sebastian.
10. One of the two border fortresses guarding the northern entry to Portugal which fell to the French on 27 July, 1810. A mortar bomb hit the garrison magazine producing an explosion which wrecked the town and killed some 500 Portuguese soldiers. Masséna was now free to advance. Wellington waited for him at Busaco, a splendid defensive position on a hill not far from Coimbra.
11. i.e. close to
12. His firelock or musket
13. presumably Leyria
14. i.e. The major on duty at the time.
15. Wellington
16. Presumably this was Leith
17. Andrew Hay
18. Later Major General Sir Dudley St Leger Hill. A former officer of the 95th Rifles (The Rifle Brigade), he was one of those appointed by Beresford to a company in the Portuguese Army and served on in it until 1820. He had a fine fighting record and was wounded no

less than seven times in the Peninsula. He died whilst commanding a division in Bengal in 1851.

19. Properly Caçadores.
20. The Portuguese royal house, dating from 1640.
21. It may happen that several towns are not properly spelt. *Author's Note*
22. The Provost Marshal
23. i.e. The trail of powder laid to act as a fuze for the explosives
24. In addition to those in the KGL, there were quite a number of Germans serving in the Army in various units.
25. This reference to Oliver Goldsmith's poem *The Deserted Village* is yet another indication of the width of Douglas's reading.
26. Milton's *Paradise Lost*.
27. i.e. from the dead bodies of the French soldiers strewn along the route.
28. A name given by the soldiers for a bad shirt, *Author's Note*; i.e. it was infested with lice.
29. 17 March.
30. The steady flow of Irish Catholic recruits was vital to the survival of Wellington's army in the Peninsula. In 1810 the Irish content of the Army was about forty per cent. They were a mixed blessing, as Correlli Barnett explains in his *Britain and Her Army 1509–1970*: 'Although they were hardy and brave, they were also ignorant, mad for drink, violent and without self discipline'.
31. A piece of chewing tobacco.
32. Major General (later Lieutenant General) James Dunlop. Formerly a brigade commander in the 5th Division, he assumed command of the Division when Leith went home on sick leave (see Note 9). The Dictionary of National Biography records that 'when the division went into winter quarters, Dunlop obtained leave of absence and did not rejoin the Peninsular Army. Although he was promoted Lieutenant General in 1814, the fact that he did not go back to the Peninsula and received no honours for that campaign, suggests, as Douglas implies, that Dunlop had incurred Wellington's displeasure for his failure at Sabugal.
33. The steelyard was a form of balance with a short arm to take the item to be weighed and a long one along which a weight was moved to achieve a balance.
34. The intention seems to have been to ensure that, should a soldier die or be killed, there would be sufficient funds in his account to cater for any debts and so avoid the burden of settlement falling on the funds of his company.

35. i.e. dishonest trading with the local population.
36. old hands
37. i.e. he was repaid in the base coinage hidden in the soldier's pocket.
38. This paragraph appears later in Douglas's narrative but is included here to preserve continuity of his observations on the subject.

3. Fuentes de Oñoro, Badajoz and Salamanca

1. Properly, Fuentes de Oñoro
2. Douglas's contempt for the Spanish Army was shared by every member of Wellington's forces, from his Lordship down. Although a formidable force on paper, it was, in truth, the feeblest and most unreliable of all Britain's allies in the Peninsula. Wellington described the Spanish as children in the art of war who could only perform efficiently in one respect, 'running away and assembling again in a state of nature'. Surtees of the 95th described their officers as 'the most contemptible creatures I ever beheld' and their soldiers 'on their best days are more like an armed mob than regularly organized soldiers'. Even their fellow Iberians, the Portuguese, would jeer at them. However, there were some twenty-two 'foreign' regiments on their strength – mostly Swiss and Irish – who certainly showed more enthusiasm for battle and who, when serving under Wellington's direct command, as at Albuera, fought very well. Of all the Spanish troops the artillery were probably the best. Time and again they suffered heavy losses when defending their guns after their infantry had fled.

   In direct contrast was the major contribution to the Allied cause made by the bands of civilian guerrillas who harassed the French in ruthless partisan warfare inflicting the most terrible cruelties upon them – so well depicted in Goya's series of sketches entitled 'Horrors of War'. Needless to say, the French repaid them in the same coinage.
3. Here Douglas is presumably referring to men of the foreign regiments.
4. The escape of the garrison created much adverse criticism, not least from Wellington himself. In addition to putting the principal blame on General Campbell (see the Historical Note on page 31), he was particularly critical of Lieutenant Colonel Cochrane of the 36th Foot who had rashly crossed the bridge over the River Agueda and was sharply checked by elements of Reynier's 2nd Corps. Above all he censured Lieutenant Colonel Charles Bevan, commanding the 4th Foot, whose failure to reach his position in time had allowed

the French to escape. He had received orders before midnight to march to Barba de Puerco, but, being reluctant to rouse his soldiers, who had only just bedded down, he delayed this move until daylight. Tragically, Wellington's censure hit him so hard that he committed suicide on 8 July.

Great credit must go the French for their skilled and very well disciplined escape and especially to Comte Antoine-François Brennier, their commander, who was promoted to *général de division* not long after.

5. Where the hospital was located.
6. A wolf.
7. Cremona. A town in Italy surprised by Prince Eugene. By their swift reaction, the Irish Brigade under his command saved the town as the French arrived almost as soon as it had fallen.
8. Units which had served in the Egyptian campaign of 1801 had the emblem of the Sphinx over the word 'Egypt' emblazoned upon the regimental colour and some had it incorporated in their cap badge or collar badges.
9. i.e. excused two picquet duties.
10. 25 September, 1811
11. A civilian official of the Commissariat. This organization was under Treasury control, not under that of the Army. It was responsible for the logistic support of the Army in the field and the transportation, by supply column, of every form of military necessity, including ammunition. Delivery was mainly by ox cart and so terribly slow. Both the carts and their drivers were hired locally and a constant source of trouble. Douglas explains how, often, the Commissariat was many miles behind the marching troops, who consequently suffered extremes of hunger and were desperately short of such things as new shoes and clothing. Nevertheless, the function of the Commissariat was a vital element in Wellington's success, for the French had nothing like it and struggled to live off a barren countryside which, as at Torres Vedras, had been stripped bare on Wellington's orders. The shortage of foodstuffs and the constant harassment by the guerrillas made the life of the French soldier a misery. For all its faults, the Commissariat worked and enabled Wellington to have the strategic mobility that allowed him to march all over Spain and Portugal as he wished. As for the Commissaries themselves, they were a very mixed lot. many were inefficient and corrupt, and their superiors were often little better, but many others did their willing best despite the toils of bureaucracy and harassment by ignorant officers. It was a thankless task, made no easier by the

abuse often heaped upon the Commissaries of all ranks by the troops and their senior officers, but the truth is that it was a campaign winner.

12. Ciudad Rodrigo was originally captured by Marshal Ney in July, 1810. Now, two years later, Wellington could besiege it almost without enemy interference because the bulk of the French were in eastern Spain under Marshal Suchet. The fortress fell on 19 January, 1812.

13. The trenches were created parallel to the walls of the beseiged fortress and moved progressively towards them.

14. i.e. capable of being stormed. When a breach was deemed to be practicable, the garrison could surrender without loss of honour.

15. He had returned from sick leave in England (see Chapter 2 Note 9) and reassumed command of the division during the final stages of the siege.

16. Blown up by the defence.

17. The Baker rifle, with which the rifle regiments and some of the KGL were equipped, as opposed to the Brown Bess of the line regiments.

18. The tot was a measure, usually made of horn, carried by the soldier in which he drew his rum ration.

19. Due to the number of musket balls being fired at them.

20. The main breach.

21. i.e. whether or not the house was occupied.

22. His tobacco pipe

23. The French

24. Wellington

25. His Spanish firelock

26. The French forts at Salamanca surrendered on 27 June, 1812.

27. Wellington. *Author's Footnote*

28. The 5th Dragoon Guards. So called because of their green cavalry overalls (close-fitting trousers).

29. The term 'brigade' was then applied to a battery of six guns.

30. 5th Dragoon Guards.

31. Marshal Auguste Frédéric Louis Viesse de Marmont first came to Napoleon's notice at the siege of Toulon in 1793. Both served there as artillery officers, Napoleon making his name there and starting on his road to fame. When he became a general, he made Marmont his ADC, a moment from which Marmont never looked back. He soon became one of Napoleon's best commanders and was made a Marshal of France after Wagram in 1809. Having replaced Masséna as commander of the Army of Portugal after Fuentes de Oñoro (see Historical Note on page 32), he had little success against the British

and was severely wounded in the arm at Salamanca but returned to duty in Germany in 1813 to command the VIth Corps, with which he achieved much. However, he deserted Napoleon by surrendering his corps to the Allies outside Paris in 1814 for which he was instantly dismissed. Honoured by Louis XVIII after the Restoration, he then had a somewhat chequered career which led to his exile after the revolution in 1830, when he was again accused of treachery.

32. Melas was the Austrian commander defeated by Napoleon at Marengo in June, 1800. Like Marmont, he was wounded in the arm. Here again we have evidence of Douglas's wide knowledge of history.

33. The British soldiers.

34. 'God be merciful unto me a sinner'. *Luke, Chapter 18 v. 13*

35. The Portuguese line regiments were numbered from 1–24.

36. This reference is obscure but it seems likely that he was referring to the mounds of earth built in public parks to protect spectators during archery contests which were very popular on public holidays in such places.

37. Arrogant and boastful. A term coined from the character Braggadochio in Spenser's *Fairie Queene*.

38. Three regiments of heavy cavalry.

39. The Portuguese.

40. The British skirmishers, having pursued their French counterparts, were blocking the fire of the rifle companies, so their recall was imperative.

41. The Eagle was the French equivalent of the British Regimental Colour. Presented to each regiment on parade by Napoleon himself, the loss of an Eagle was deemed an unforgiveable failure by the Emperor.

42. A former Spanish monarch.

43. Correctly, El Escorial. Philip II (1527–98) created this huge edifice which combines the features of a monastery and a palace. He established it as the royal mausoleum.

44. This remark seems to suggest that Douglas wrote his Tale whilst still of military age but the actual date is unknown.

4. Burgos: The Siege is Raised and We Retreat

1. By capturing Burgos, Wellington had hoped to capture both Soult and King Joseph as well.

2. See Historical Note above.

3. i.e. make out a strength state.

4. We know from Chapter 5 (see page 86) that Douglas was still a Corporal at this time. As the only full rank NCO left in the Company he was having to carry out the duties of what we would now call the Company Sergeant Major but who was then the senior Sergeant, the only Sergeant Major in the Battalion being the equivalent of today's Regimental Sergeant Major.

5. Patching.

6. i.e. To ensure that any of the local peasantry who sought to steal the rum were dealt with.

7. Made something like our own sausages, but as thick as a man's arm. They were very good with the exception of that ingredient with which all their dishes are seasoned; viz garlick [sic]. *Author's Note*

8. A league was about three miles.

9. Father Mathew. A famous Catholic priest who was a leader of the temperance movement. The fact that he did not sign the pledge until 1838 and achieved his greatest fame in the 1840s give us another clue to the date upon which Douglas's Tale was written.

10. Thou shalt not steal.

11. Lieutenant Colonel Colin Campbell. Appointed a Major in Douglas's battalion in September, 1810, he was now the acting Commanding Officer, having been awarded a brevet promotion on 17 August, 1812. He acted in this capacity at several critical points in the battalion's history – Salamanca, Vitoria, Quatre Bras and Waterloo, where he particularly distinguished himself.

12. At this time the Corps of Royal Engineers was essentially an all-officer corps. The rank and file for engineering duties were provided either by the Royal Military Artificers, a small corps of builders, carpenters and artificers whose primary duty was the maintenance of fortresses and fixed defences and officered by its own officers, who were not trained engineers, or from unskilled volunteers drawn from the line regiments. None of these men were skilled in siege warfare and, in any case, the number of Military Artificers in Wellington's army was very small – only about 100 men up to 1811. It was not until Wellington sent a vehement letter to Lord Liverpool after the heavy casualties suffered at Badajoz, which he attributed largely to the paucity and inadequacy of his engineer support, that a new corps, the Royal Sappers and Miners, commanded by Royal Engineers and trained in field engineering at Chatham, was formed. By 1813 some 300 Sappers and Miners were available in the Peninsula. These performed yeoman service at San Sebastian, as we shall see in Chapter 5.

13. Few armies in history can have marched as Wellington's did in the Peninsula and how this was achieved with the boots then issued to the soldier is hard to imagine. Douglas refers more than once to the problem of men going barefoot because their boots had disintegrated due to the going and the weather conditions and in this chapter we find him going into hospital himself with a serious foot condition, clearly the byproduct of the long marches. Known as 'shoes' to differentiate them from the long boots of the cavalry, the infantryman's boot was designed to be worn on either foot and he was ordered to wear his boots on alternate feet to stop them getting out of shape. If well repaired, a pair of boots in general use was expected to last a year, but under the conditions of the Peninsula they would need replacing much sooner than that. Indeed, on occasions special free issues were made because of the hard wear to which the men's boots had been subjected. When the Commissariat's stocks of British boots ran out, locally made substitutes were issued which were far from satisfactory. So it is easy to see how important the company cobblers were. Rifleman John Harris of the 95th Rifles has described his work as a cobbler in his well-known memoir *Recollections of Rifleman Harris* edited by H. Curling (Peter Davies, London 1929).

14. Of tobacco.

15. The soldiers' name for the small pack artillery pieces used by the Spanish guerrillas, usually 3prs.

16. He fell afterwards at San Sebastian. *Author's Note*

17. Major General (later General Sir John) Oswald, in temporary command of the 5th Division during the absence of Sir John Leith and remaining in command until the army went into winter quarters. Resuming command in May, 1813, he commanded the division at Vitoria and through the greater part of the seige of San Sebastian until relieved by Leith on 31 August. Oswald returned to brigade command but both men were wounded on that same day and command passed to Major General Andrew Hay, who, it will be remembered was Douglas's former Commanding Officer.

18. The Royal Scots

19. A very common observation of his. *Author's Note*

20. See Note 13 in which the question of footwear is explained.

21. Presumably the name of an inn familiar to the Author.

22. General Hill (later 1st Viscount) and one of Wellington's most trusted and distinguished corps commanders. From 1815–18 he would serve as Wellington's second-in-command in the Army of Occupation.

23. See Historical Note on page 52. Hill was heading for Arevalo where the stocks of new clothing were to be sent.
24. 'the Land of Nod, on the East of Eden', *Genesis* Ch. 4 v. 16
25. Transport
26. Officers' servants.
27. The Foot Guards, all three regiments of whom had battalions serving in the Peninsula.
28. The rations.
29. Gangrenous.
30. A nice touch of irony, for McGowan was one of the drunken soldiers he had been told to escort during the retreat from Burgos and thanks to whom he had been cut off from his battalion and very nearly captured by the French (see pages 54–5).

5. The Battle of Vitoria and Siege of San Sebastian
1. General Graham (See Chapter 1 Note 10)
2. This presumably refers to the recent recruiting drive to persuade soldiers to extend their service (See Chapter 4 pages 67–8). The Government's half of the deal was a bounty in cash. The soldier's half was the risk of losing his life or being disabled in battle.
3. The implication of this remark being that there would be so many casualties that day that there would be no shortage of rations for those who survived.
4. Although using the word 'tumbrel', he clearly means the ammunition limber of the gun.
5. The word 'doubloon' was widely used since Elizabethan times to denote the Spanish-American gold pieces that flooded Europe in the 16th–18th Centuries. Douglas's doubloon would have been the Spanish gold escudo.
6. By no means the most insignificant prize was King Joseph's own carriage, found to be crammed with the most precious spoils from the churches and palaces of Spain. Some of the finest paintings of the Spanish masters were found in the baggage train – along with some of the King's attractive female companions.
7. Pasta
8. The term 'conductor' was used for a Warrant Officer responsible for the supervision of the transportation by land or water of stores, equipment and ammunition to magazines, arsenals and depots. A conductor would be attached either to the ordnance or the Commissariat Departments. The term lives on today as a title for Warrant Officers Class I in the Royal Logistic Corps fulfilling certain functions. In this instance, Corporal Teal was clearly deputising for

a conductor and had been loaned by Douglas's battalion for the purpose.

9. The Adjutant was addressing Corporal Teal who, it will be remembered was an old adversary of Douglas's (see Chapter 3 page 32).

10. A term (or name) used in the Army for those who were flogged. *Author's Note.*

11. The Provost Marshal (See Chapter 2 Note 22).

12. A brave soldier, he afterwards fell at Quatre Bras, 16th June 1815. *Author's Note*

13. The castle of San Sebastian stands high on a steep hill, and is a complete peninsula. *Author's Note*
    There were, in fact, two French batteries, one on each side of the castle of La Mota. The signal post mentioned by Douglas on page 80 was sited to the right of one of these batteries. The town of San Sebastian stands on a low-lying peninsula which juts out from north to south of the mainland for some 11,000 yards. At its end is a rugged hill, about 400 feet high, named Monte Orgullo.

14. 'The first law of nature'. In this context, Douglas must mean the instinct for survival. It is interesting to note how inured the troops had become to such hazardous and trying conditions. It has to be remembered that many of them were battle-hardened veterans who had endured extremes of hardship and danger over many months. Douglas remarks more than once on the few men who survived from the new drafts and how the draft of 250 received after Salamanca were quite at sea when faced by severe weather conditions and a route that had become a morass.

15. i.e. began to dig new entrenchments as part of the technique of siege warfare then in vogue. (see Chapter 3 Note 13).

16. See Chapter 3 Note 14.

17. The term 'curtain' refers here to the high ramparts encompassing the perimeter of the defences. Emanuel Ray, the French commander of the fortress, had created a wall fifteen feet high by building up on the ruins of the houses already destroyed in the bombardment, using the rubble from the top stories. The drop to the street on the inside was as much as twenty feet in places.

18. His face would have been covered by new skin and scar tissue from the burns he had received at San Sebastian.

19. A British frigate and nineteen smaller vessels had been blockading San Sebastian harbour since 8 July but were unable to prevent the French blockade runners from St Jean de Luz from slipping through the net in the hours of darkness.

20. Monte Orgullo (see Note 13 above).

21. The forlorn hope was the spearhead of the storming party. Despite the extremely hazardous nature of the task, which often involved the use of scaling ladders, there was never any shortage of volunteers for the forlorn hope. Should he survive (and all too often he did not) the officer leading it could be assured of fame and welcome recognition of his gallantry. The story usually referred to as *Dyas and the Stormers* at Badajoz is part of the fabric of British military history and is admirably described by Private Wheeler of Dyas's regiment (51st Light Infantry, later the King's Own Yorkshire Light Infantry) in *The Letters of Private Wheeler 1809–1829* edited by Captain B. H. Liddell Hart (Michael Joseph, 1951).

22. The word 'aerial' as we now understand it would have been virtually unknown in general use. Douglas must be using the metaphor of the Shakespearean spirit in *The Tempest* – yet another indication of his broad-based reading and good education.

23. See Note 19.

24. This rather obscure reference must be taken to refer to the work of the surgeons in patching up the wounded and making amputations, thereby preparing the soldiers for acceptance as permanently disabled veterans in The Royal Hospital, Chelsea.

25. Musket balls coated with a poisonous substance.

26. Tetanus.

27. A medical orderly working on the ward.

28. i.e. bribe him.

29. George Cruikshank was a famous cartoonist and illustrator, best known for his illustrations of Dickens' novels and the works of other leading novelists of the day including Thackeray, the Brothers Grimm and Sir Walter Scott. Cruikshank had a brother with whom he also worked. The use of the plural here might mean that Douglas was referring to both men.

30. Surgeon's assistants, some of whom were actually qualified as doctors and were starting their way up the ladder of promotion to assistant surgeon, surgeon and staff surgeon but many, as Rogers tells us, had few qualifications and the examination standards for acceptance were low so that many surgeon's or hospital mates were men of poor education and inadequate medical knowledge (HCB Rogers, *Wellington's Army* (Ian Allan, 1979)).

31. Douglas is referring here to the portable, prefabricated hospital buildings introduced by James McGrigor, a great humanitarian who was appointed Inspector General of Hospitals. His mobile hospitals marked a major step forward in medical care as they could keep up

with movements of the troops in the field. Until they were introduced, the wounded suffered agonies as they were transported over long distances in unsprung wooden carts – many dying en route to the hospitals at the base.

32. Douglas must mean the surgeon in charge of the hospital for there were no doctors holding the rank of General at that time, nor was there a formal medical organization with any rank structure as in the Royal Army Medical Corps today.

33. This rather unexpected observation suggests that Douglas had read a distinguished history of the conquest of Mexico by Cortes in the 16th Century, written by an American named William Hickling Prescott and published in 1843. As with the reference to Father Mathew (see Chapter 4 Note 9), this suggests that Douglas did not write his Tale until the late 1840s. It is yet another pointer to the breadth of his reading and suggests that he continued to read widely after he had left the Army.

34. Properly Master-at-Arms. This post was often filled by a former Army NCO whose principal duty was to train the sailors in small arms drill but who also had some part in the maintenance of discipline. The title lives on in the Royal Navy today and is the naval equivalent of the Army's Provost Sergeant. Although the Master-at-Arms was appointed by the Admiralty and so was rated as a Warrant Officer (i.e. he held an Admiralty Warrant) he was a fairly lowly person in a ships hierarchy of Warrant Officers, and well below such 'sea officers' as the Master (or navigator) or Boatswain.

35. Douglas gives us no indication who this choleric gentleman actually was but the fact that he had his own coach and was recognized by the soldier of the 78th Regiment who shouted out at him suggests that he was Lord Blaney, responsible for one of the most disgraceful episodes in the Peninsular War, when a force under his command was utterly routed by the French when it attempted to sieze the port of Malaga in 1810.

36. Douglas is referring here to the closure of the continental ports to British trade by the Berlin Decree of 21 November, 1806, thus implementing Napoleon's 'continental System'. All ships were searched for British contraband. It was Portugal's refusal to observe this convention that led to the French invasion of the country and to Portugal's appeal to Britain for help in 1807 (see Historical Note for Chapter 2 on page 13).

37. Argus was a mythical Greek figure with 100 eyes.

38. Douglas clearly means the rocky coast of the Scilly Isles.

6. The Waterloo Campaign

1. See Chapter 4 Note 11.
2. Received no pension or gratuity.
3. Women
4. Money
5. Green forage was the name given to our suppers which generally consisted of salads. *Author's Note*
6. Probably from Ligny (see Historical Note on page 94).
7. i.e. properly secured in the hammer.
8. Heavy cavalry.
9. Lieutenant General Sir Thomas Picton, one of the truly great fighting generals in the history of the British Army. General Officer Commanding 3rd Division (known for its prowess in battle as the Iron Division), he was a professional to his fingertips and a strict disciplinarian with a colourful flow of language. After Badajoz, at which he led the assault on the breach himself, he awarded a guinea to each man of the division who survived. He himself had been severely wounded. Of his conduct at the siege, Lord Liverpool paid him this tribute in the House of Lords:

   > The conduct of General Picton has inspired confidence in the army and exhibited an example of science and bravery which has been surpassed by no other officer.

   He led his division from success to success throughout the campaign, returning from sick leave, after a bout of fever which had prevented him from commanding at Salamanca, to win fresh triumphs. Seriously wounded at Waterloo, he concealed the fact and continued to fight until a musket ball struck him in the head and killed him.
10. The 28th Regiment and the Royal Scots.
11. A hackle, which was a symbol of special achievement and gallantry in battle and worn in the cap or highland bonnet.
12. i.e. that the British would be heading for their ships and return to England.
13. The old hulks in which the British kept their prisoners of war at that time.
14. In 1815 Belgium did not exist as a separate state and the term 'Belgian' was little used. Until 1814 Belgium had merely been a part of the Austrian Netherlands, which had been united in that year with the Republic of Holland, so it is possible that Douglas was referring to the Netherlands units as a whole in this instance. Although he and his comrades had a poor opinion of the fighting qualities of the Netherlands troops, often remarking how many men

seemed to accompany each wounded man to the rear, it has to be said that the two Nassau regiments, who until quite recently had been serving Napoleon in Spain, fought with great courage and determination at Waterloo, still dressed in the green uniforms they had worn in the Peninsula. With the advent of Belgian independence in 1830, the term 'Belgian' became generally used. Here we have yet another pointer to the date at which Douglas's Tale was written.

15. Wellington had learned the value of the reverse slope position in the Peninsula. As Blücher's rejection of his advice and subsequent fatal error at Ligny showed, Wellington was ahead of much military thinking in this respect (see Historical Note on page 94).

16. See Note 9 above.

17. i.e. The British guns, being forward of the infantry squares, had to be left in position whilst the gunners sheltered in the squares during a cavalry attack, leaving the guns to the mercy of the enemy who, fortunately, were in no position to take advantage of the situation.

18. McDonald was a Captain in the Royal Scots holding brevet rank as a Major and detached to Brigade Headquarters. Clearly, he had realized that the battalion had lost all its officers and had come to take command. During the battles of Quatre Bras and Waterloo, the 3rd Royal Scots lost seven officers killed and fourteen wounded.

19. Griffiths was harking back to the time of Badajoz when, as a Quartermaster Sergeant, he had been involved in an altercation over rations with the Quartermaster of the 78th Regiment. This had led to his reduction to the ranks by Court Martial. However, when the Colonel of the Regiment, Field Marshal the Duke of Kent, heard of this, he immediately ordered that Griffiths should be restored in rank. The battalion Quartermaster retired a few months later and Griffiths was commissioned in his place. The Duke took an immense interest in the wellbeing of the regiment and its officers who regarded him as a valued friend and counsellor.

20. In the original text, this paragraph appears as a footnote. It has been inserted here as it adds an interesting human touch to Douglas's account of the battle.

21. La Belle Alliance was an inn that, for much of the battle, was in the centre of the French position. It was from this area that Napoleon fled at the end of the battle to find his coach at Genappe. It was, of course, also the place at which Wellington met Blücher as the pursuit began, Blücher observing, in what Wellington used to say were his only words of French, 'Quelle affaire!'

22. A pension.

23. Le Cateau.
24. i.e. having a good excuse to get into Paris in order to show the orders to their officers.
25. For all his education, Douglas had a typical soldier's sense of humour, as is so evident throughout his Tale. Without it, it is doubtful whether a man could have survived all that he went through on campaign.
26. The book containing Regimental Orders (and hence not a book to be mislaid).
27. The British Foreign Secretary from 1812–22 who played a leading part in the Congress of Vienna, which redrew the map of Europe in 1814–15.
28. Manoeuvres put on as a spectacle.
29. In such circumstances the men's muskets would have been loaded with a charge of powder only. This, when fired, would have given a flame that would have enabled the soldier to see briefly where he was going or might have been used as a guide for others following the firer through the swamp in the dark.
30. A perch was five and a half yards.
31. Bouchain surrendered to Marlborough on 14 September, 1711. In December he was dismissed for misuse of public funds. There seems to be little doubt that it was a trumped-up charge laid by the Tories in the House of Commons. They were opposed to the continuation of the War of the Spanish Succession and wished to see Marlborough removed from the post of Commander of the Grand Alliance against Louis XIV.
32. It is remarkable to record that Wellington drafted forgers into the ranks of the Peninsular Army to produce forged Spanish and Portuguese currency in order to enable him to overcome the effects of the extreme stringency of the funding by the British Government from London. Sir John Moore found himself in the same position during the Corunna Campaign but did not indulge in such practices – to have done so would have been totally out of character. Wellington was a much more pragmatic man and nothing was allowed to come between him and the proper conduct of operations if he could possibly help it. Doubtless, this man was one of those forgers and had been putting his skills to his own advantage.

Select Bibliography

Designed to give the reader access to greater detail of the Peninsular and Waterloo Campaigns and of the organization, equipment and tactics of the British Army in Douglas's time, with particular reference to Wellington's army in the Peninsula.

Barnett, Correlli. *Britain and Her Army 1509–1970* (1984)
Brandon, A. M. *The Royal Scots* (1976)
Brett-James, A. ed. *Adventures of a Soldier*, Edward Costello
Bryant, Sir Arthur. *The Great Duke* (1971)
Chandler, D. *Dictionary of the Napoleonic Wars* (1979)
Curling, H. ed. *The Recollections of Rifleman Harris* (1929)
Glover, M. *Wellington's Army* (1977)
Haythornthwaite, P. J. *British Infantry in the Napoleonic Wars* (1987)
    Weapons and Equipment of the Napoleonic Wars (1987)
    Wellington's Military Machine (1989)
Kincaid, J. *Adventures in the Rifle Brigade* (1830)
    Random Shots of a Rifleman (1847)
Liddell Hart, B. H. ed. *The Letters of Private Wheeler 1809–1828* (1951)
Ludovic, A. M. ed. *On the Road with Wellington*, A. E. F. Schaumann (1924)
Oman, Sir Charles. *History of the Peninsular War* (7 vols) (1902–30)
    Wellington's Army (1912)
Rogers, H. C. B. *Wellington's Army* (1979)
Ward, S. P. G. *Wellington's Headquarters* (1957)
Weller, J. *Wellington in the Peninsula* (1962)
    Wellington and Waterloo (1967)

Index

132